THE COMPLETE JAZZ GUITAR

Written and Arranged by
FRED SOKOLOW

Edited by Ronny Schiff & Norman Schwartz
Internal Graphics by Mary Francis

# INTRODUCTION

Jazz is a sophisticated art form with an evolutionary history spanning more than a century. From its primitive beginnings to its complexities today, jazz has placed increasing emphasis on the role of the guitarist.

In early jazz bands the guitarist supplied rhythmic and chordal support for the soloists. But with the advent of electric guitar and Charlie Christian's influence, the guitarist became a prominent soloist. Guitar improvisations became as fundamental as horn or keyboard solos. Now, in a time of jazz-rock "fusion", the guitar player is a leading voice in jazz.

Today's jazz guitarist must know how to use chords, both for back-up as well as soloing, and he or she must know how to solo in the "single note" style. This book explains the theory and practice of:

CHORDS... How they are constructed; how they function in progressions; how they can be substituted and varied; and finally, how to play chord solos and chordal accompaniment.

SINGLE NOTE SOLOING... How and when to play different scales; how to practice scales; how to improvise "single string" and "octave" solos over chord progressions.

To put theory into practice, a dozen "sample" solos are presented, many of them important mainline jazz tunes. These solos are professionally played on a cassette recording. The reader can follow along with each solo which is written out in both standard music notation and tablature with chord grids. The "ear musician" and the reading musician will find that this presentation accommodates different styles of learning and playing.

Some sections contain technical information that may seem difficult to assimilate at one time. These sections—the chord dictionary, the scale exercises, chapters on chord and scale substitution, etc.—are nonetheless useful as reference. Always check back for new playing ideas.

All the necessary material is here for the do-it-yourself student or for the teacher of jazz guitar. I believe that many proficient jazz guitarists will enjoy this book as well, and may find it helpful.

Fred Sokolow

CONTENTS

HOW TO READ THE TABLATURE

The music in this book is written both in tablature and standard music notation. Use either system.

In tablature, the 6 lines on the staff represent the 6 strings of the guitar, as follows:

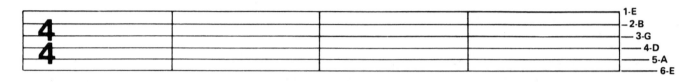

A number on a line indicates where to fret the string.

This example: means "play the 4th string on the 2nd fret."

This example: means "play the 2nd string unfretted."

Many left hand techniques are indicated in tablature:

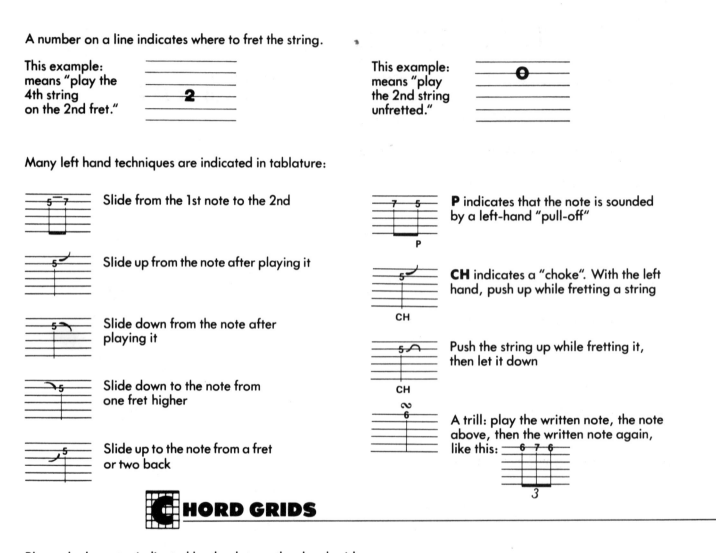

Slide from the 1st note to the 2nd

Slide up from the note after playing it

Slide down from the note after playing it

Slide down to the note from one fret higher

Slide up to the note from a fret or two back

P indicates that the note is sounded by a left-hand "pull-off"

CH indicates a "choke". With the left hand, push up while fretting a string

Push the string up while fretting it, then let it down

A trill: play the written note, the note above, then the written note again, like this:

CHORD GRIDS

Play only the notes indicated by the dots on the chord grid.

In this example: C11 do not play the 6th or 4th strings.

The fret number is shown to the right of the chord. Where there is no fret number, as in the example above, fret the chord as pictured (on the 1st fret).

This chord: F11 6 is to be played on the 6th fret, like this:

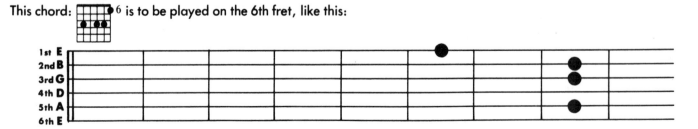

 **HORDS**

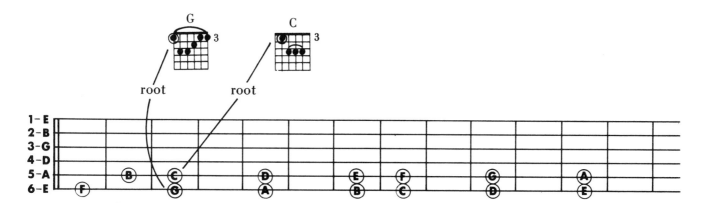

The two chords, G and C, and the fingerboard chart above, form the basis for a solid understanding of *chord types*.

The "root" of the G chord is the G note that gives the chord its name. It lies on the 6th string.

The G chord formation is moveable. Played with the root at the 5th fret, like this: 5 it is an A chord.

At the 6th fret: 6 it is a B♭ chord, and so on.

The root of the C chord is the C note on the 5th string. Move the formation down two frets like this:
and it is a B♭ chord, since the 5th string on the 1st fret is B♭.

Play the formation on the 7th fret: 7 and it is an E chord.

These two chord formations offer two ways to play *any major chord*. Simply fret the chord with the root on the desired note.

For example, here are two E♭ chords (two different *voicings* of the same chord):

To practice these two formations, and to **memorize** the notes on the 5th and 6th string,
play two different voicings of these chords: C♯, B, D, A♭, F

INTERVALS

An interval is the distance in pitch between two notes. Each chord type (major, minor, etc.) is made up of certain intervals. Variations in chords are made by adding or changing intervals.

Look at the C scale on the fingerboard:

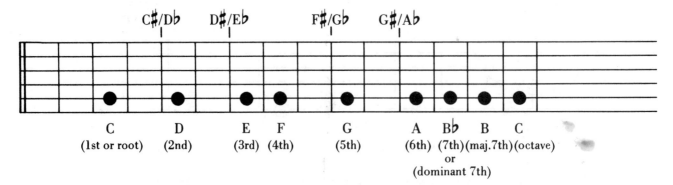

Every note in the scale is assigned a number. Intervals are described by those numbers. In a C scale, C is the "1st" or root. D is the 2nd interval, or simply the "2nd." E is the "3rd," F is the "4th," and so on. B is the "major 7th" while Bb (A#) is the "dominant 7th" or 7th. C above B is the 8th, more commonly called the "octave." D above C is the 9th.

The pattern of intervals is the same for every major scale. In the key of D, D is the 1st. The 2nd (E) is 2 frets above D, the 3rd (F#) is 2 frets above the 2nd. The 4th (G) is *one* fret above the 3rd. The general rule is: *all intervals are a "whole step" (two frets) apart except the 4th (a half-step—one fret—above the 3rd) and the octave (a half-step—one fret—above the major 7th).*

No matter what the starting note, the pattern of intervals remains the same. If F is the 1st (6th string, 1st fret), then G, 2 frets higher, is the 2nd; A, 2 frets above G, is the 3rd; Bb, 1 fret above A, is the 4th. Following this pattern, the octave note—F—lies on the 13th fret.

Try to find a 3rd, 4th, 5th, or any interval above a fixed starting note. Answer the questions below using the guitar fingerboard as a reference.

1) What note lies a 3rd above G? A 6th above G? A 9th above G?
2) What note lies a 4th above E? A 3rd above E? A 5th above E?
3) If Bb is the 1st, what is the 2nd? The 4th? The dominant 7th?

ANSWERS: 1) B, E, A 2) A, G#, B 3) C, Eb, Ab

CHORD CONSTRUCTION

Chord construction is based on intervals.

Every major chord is made up of three intervals, the 1st, 3rd and 5th. Thus, a C chord is C, E, and G in any combination. The barred C chord below contains (from bass to treble strings): C, G, C, E.

A G chord is G, B and D, the 1st, 3rd and 5th in the key of G. The barred chord shown contains 3 G's, 2 D's and a B.

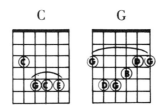

MAJOR CHORD VARIATIONS

In each of these variations, the familiar major chord (1, 3, 5) changes slightly as a new interval is added. The composition of each new chord is described in intervals. For example, the first variation, the "dominant 7th", is a major chord (1, 3, 5) with a dominant 7th added.

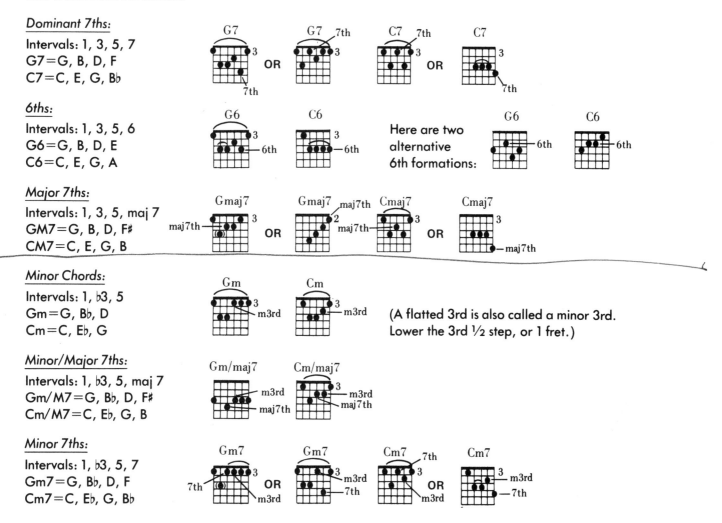

Dominant 7ths:
Intervals: 1, 3, 5, 7
G7 = G, B, D, F
C7 = C, E, G, B♭

6ths:
Intervals: 1, 3, 5, 6
G6 = G, B, D, E
C6 = C, E, G, A

Here are two alternative 6th formations:

Major 7ths:
Intervals: 1, 3, 5, maj 7
GM7 = G, B, D, F♯
CM7 = C, E, G, B

Minor Chords:
Intervals: 1, ♭3, 5
Gm = G, B♭, D
Cm = C, E♭, G

(A flatted 3rd is also called a minor 3rd. Lower the 3rd ½ step, or 1 fret.)

Minor/Major 7ths:
Intervals: 1, ♭3, 5, maj 7
Gm/M7 = G, B♭, D, F♯
Cm/M7 = C, E♭, G, B

Minor 7ths:
Intervals: 1, ♭3, 5, 7
Gm7 = G, B♭, D, F
Cm7 = C, E♭, G, B♭

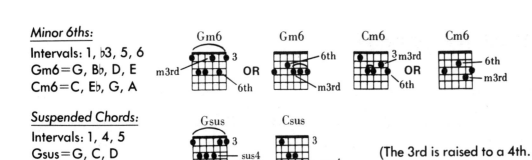

Minor 6ths:
Intervals: 1, ♭3, 5, 6
Gm6=G, B♭, D, E
Cm6=C, E♭, G, A

Gm6 — m3rd, 3, 6th
Gm6 — 6th, m3rd
OR
Cm6 — 3 m3rd, 6th
OR
Cm6 — 6th, m3rd

Suspended Chords:
Intervals: 1, 4, 5
Gsus=G, C, D
Csus=C, F, G

Gsus — 3, sus4
Csus — 3, sus4

(The 3rd is raised to a 4th.
Often called a "suspended 4th" chord.)

A suspended 4th may be added to a dominant 7th chord:

Dominant 7th Suspended:
Intervals: 1, 4, 5, 7
G7sus=G, C, D, F
C7sus=C, F, G, B♭

G7sus — 3, 7th, sus4
C7sus — 3, 7th, sus4

(Sometimes called 7th sus 4)

Augmented Chords:
Intervals: 1, 3, ♯5
G+=G, B, D♯
C+=C, E, G♯

Gaug — 3, ♯5
Caug — 4, ♯5

Here's a variation of the 1st position C chord

Caug — ♯5

(The fifth is raised a half-step)

An augmented fifth can be added to a dominant 7th chord:

Dominant 7th Augmented:
Intervals: 1, 3, ♯5, 7
G7+=G, B, D♯, F
C7+=C, E, G♯, B♭

G7(+5) — 7th, 3, ♯5
C7(+5) — 7th, 3, ♯5

These diagrams show the relative position of the major chord and its varying intervals—minors, 7ths, major 7ths, etc. The black dots indicate the original major chord formation. Listen for similarities in like chords with different roots; for example Cm6 and Gm6. Then listen for differences in chord variations with the same root; for example, C6 and Cmaj7.

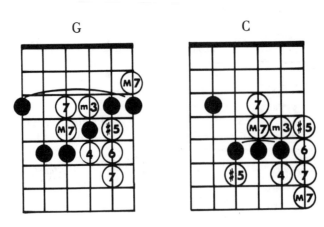

G   C

EXTENDED CHORDS

In the "extended chords" that follow—the 9ths, 11ths and 13ths—intervals that occur *above the octave* are added to the major chord and its variations. The fingerboard diagram shows however, that a 9th has the same note name as a 2nd, an 11th as a 4th, and a 13th as a 6th. When constructing chords, these "extended" intervals can be placed above or below the octave note. Also, many extended chord voicings omit an interval (for example, a 13th chord can be played without a 9th).

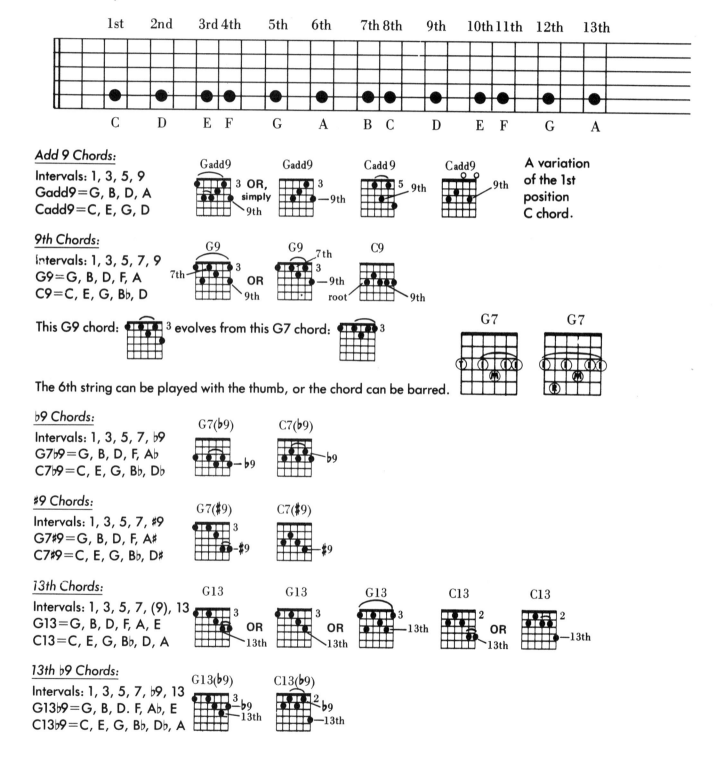

Add 9 Chords:

Intervals: 1, 3, 5, 9
Gadd9 = G, B, D, A
Cadd9 = C, E, G, D

A variation of the 1st position C chord.

9th Chords:

Intervals: 1, 3, 5, 7, 9
G9 = G, B, D, F, A
C9 = C, E, G, Bb, D

This G9 chord: evolves from this G7 chord:

The 6th string can be played with the thumb, or the chord can be barred.

b9 Chords:

Intervals: 1, 3, 5, 7, b9
G7b9 = G, B, D, F, Ab
C7b9 = C, E, G, Bb, Db

#9 Chords:

Intervals: 1, 3, 5, 7, #9
G7#9 = G, B, D, F, A#
C7#9 = C, E, G, Bb, D#

13th Chords:

Intervals: 1, 3, 5, 7, (9), 13
G13 = G, B, D, F, A, E
C13 = C, E, G, Bb, D, A

13th b9 Chords:

Intervals: 1, 3, 5, 7, b9, 13
G13b9 = G, B, D. F, Ab, E
C13b9 = C, E, G, Bb, Db, A

More +5 Chords:

Intervals: 1, 3, #5, 7, 9
G9+ = G, B, D#, F, A
C9+ = C, E, G#, Bb, D

These dominant 7th augmented chords contain 9ths, b9th or #9ths.

This chord is a variation of the 1st position C chord:

Intervals: 1, 3, #5, 7, #9
G7+5#9 = G, B, D#, F, A#
C7+5#9 = C, E, G#, Bb, D#

Intervals: 1, 3, #5, 7, b9
G7+5b9 = G, B, D#, F, Ab
C7+5b9 = C, E, G#, Bb, Db

b5 Chords:

Intervals: 1, 3, b5, 7
G7b5 = G, B, Db, F
C7b5 = D, E, Gb, Bb

Intervals: 1, 3, b5, 7, 9
G9b5 = G, B, Db, F, A
C9b5 = C, E, Gb, Bb. D

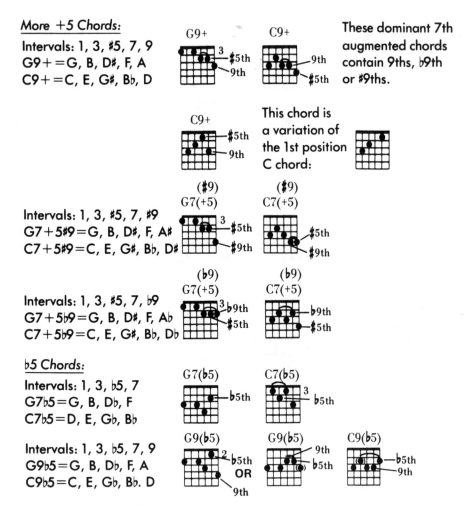

Every 7b5 chord contains the same notes as the 7b5 chord a b5th higher. For instance, C7b5 contains the same notes as Gb7b5 (Gb is a b5th above C). Therefore, every b5 chord has two names: the root and a b5 above the root.

Minor 9ths:

Intervals: 1, b5, 5, 7, 9
Gm9 = G, Bb, D, F, A
Cm9 = C, Eb, G, Bb, D

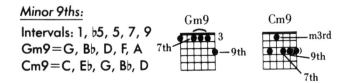

These chord charts sum up the relative position of the intervals in the "extended chords". Again, compare the sound of similar chords with different roots and disimilar chords with the same root.

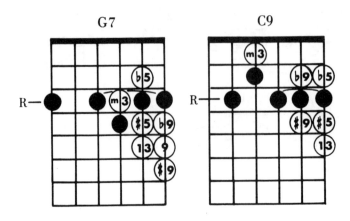

10

MORE EXTENDED CHORDS

The following chord types also have 5th or 6th string roots. They are all related to the two original major chord positions.

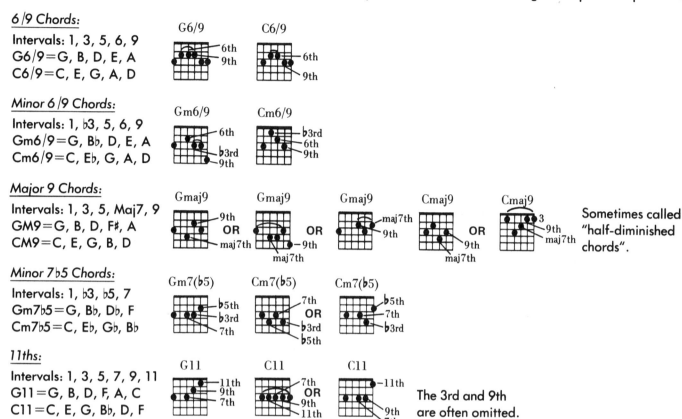

6/9 Chords:
Intervals: 1, 3, 5, 6, 9
G6/9=G, B, D, E, A
C6/9=C, E, G, A, D

G6/9   C6/9

Minor 6/9 Chords:
Intervals: 1, b3, 5, 6, 9
Gm6/9=G, Bb, D, E, A
Cm6/9=C, Eb, G, A, D

Gm6/9   Cm6/9

Major 9 Chords:
Intervals: 1, 3, 5, Maj7, 9
GM9=G, B, D, F#, A
CM9=C, E, G, B, D

Gmaj9 OR Gmaj9 OR Gmaj9   Cmaj9 OR Cmaj9

Sometimes called "half-diminished chords".

Minor 7b5 Chords:
Intervals: 1, b3, b5, 7
Gm7b5=G, Bb, Db, F
Cm7b5=C, Eb, Gb, Bb

Gm7(b5)   Cm7(b5) OR Cm7(b5)

11ths:
Intervals: 1, 3, 5, 7, 9, 11
G11=G, B, D, F, A, C
C11=C, E, G, Bb, D, F

G11   C11 OR C11

The 3rd and 9th are often omitted.

G11, as shown above, is also called F(G bass) or F/G since it contains an F major chord and a G on the bass string:

F/G

Similarly, C11 is also called Bb(C bass) or Bb/C since it has a C on the bass string and contains a Bb chord:

Bb/C

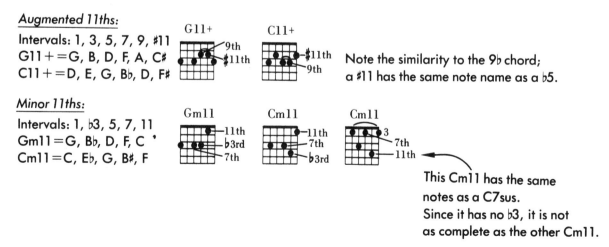

Augmented 11ths:
Intervals: 1, 3, 5, 7, 9, #11
G11+=G, B, D, F, A, C#
C11+=D, E, G, Bb, D, F#

G11+   C11+

Note the similarity to the 9b chord; a #11 has the same note name as a b5.

Minor 11ths:
Intervals: 1, b3, 5, 7, 11
Gm11=G, Bb, D, F, C
Cm11=C, Eb, G, B#, F

Gm11   Cm11   Cm11

This Cm11 has the same notes as a C7sus. Since it has no b3, it is not as complete as the other Cm11.

DiHMINISHED Chords:

Intervals: 1, ♭3, ♭5, ♭7
G°=G, B, D♭, F♭ (E)
C°=C, E♭, G♭, B♭♭ (E)

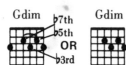

A diminished chord is a dominant seventh with every note flatted but the root. Note that a ♭7 is the same note as a 6.

Diminished chords are made up of ascending minor thirds. Since every note is a ♭3 higher than the last, the diminished chord repeats itself every three frets.

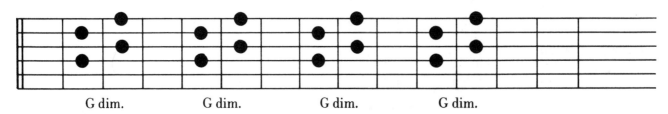

G dim.　　　G dim.　　　G dim.　　　G dim.

A diminished chord can be named by any of its notes. 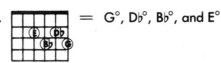 = G°, D♭°, B♭°, and E°

4TH STRING ROOT FORMATION

This chord formation is a D7 moved up two frets. Its root lies on the 4th string: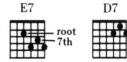

The following chords are derived from the formation below. The summary diagram shows the relative positions of the intervals. The black dots indicate the original chord.

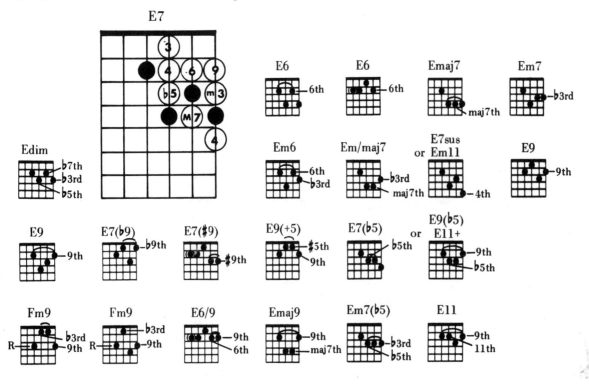

 **NVERSIONS**

In a chord inversion, a note other than the root lies on the lowest string of the formation; "inverted chords" are indispensable in chord soloing.

Chords are often written as fractions to indicate a specific bass note. For example, G (D bass) can be written: G/D.

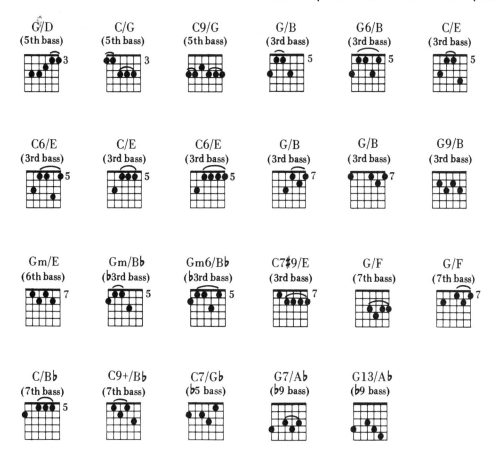

DETERMINING INTERVALS

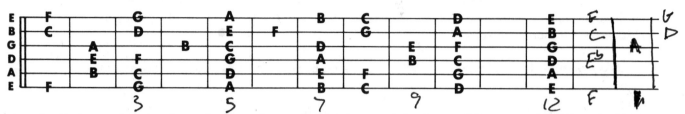

To determine the intervals in the above chords, or in any chord, it is essential to know all the notes on the fingerboard. A great deal of repetitious study is necessary to learn every note on every string. These techniques may help:

1. To learn the 5th and 6th strings, play the 5th-string root and 6th-string root major chord formations at every fret. Name each new chord that is formed.

2. The notes on the high E string (1st string) are, naturally, the same as the low E string (6th string).

3. The 4th string is a 4th higher than the 5th string. 5th string, 2nd fret is a B; 4th string, 2nd fret is, therefore, an E.

4. The 3rd string is a 4th higher than the 4th string. 4th string, 2nd fret is an E; 3rd string, 2nd fret is, therefore, an A.

5. Use octaves as shown in the diagram.

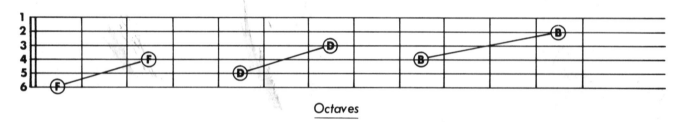

Octaves

The student that knows all the notes on the fingerboard can determine the intervals in any chord. This allows him or her to alter chords and to understand chord substitutions.

Here's how to analyze a chord for intervals, using the G9/B as an example:

First, determine the notes in the chord. They are B, F, A and D:

Now match up each of these notes with its interval in the G scale:

G	A	B	C	D	E	F	F♯	G	A
1	2	3	4	5	6	dom7	Maj7	octave	9

The intervals are: 2, 3, 5, dom7. Or: 3, 5, dom7, 9, since a 2nd has the same note name as a 9th.

14

CHORD PROGRESSIONS
THE CIRCLE OF FIFTHS

Music sets up tension and resolves it, creates expectations and fulfills it. One of the ways it does this is with chords. A chord progression is more than a series of chords strung together. Certain chords cause the listener to expect a particular chord will follow. When the expected chord is played, there is a feeling of resolution. The type of chord played, and the context in which it is played, sets up and resolves an expectation.

D7-G7-C is a resolving progression. Play the same progression without C, and feel the suspense. Without C, the progression is incomplete.

The "Circle of Fifths" diagram below is a helpful tool for understanding how chords relate in a progression. The major chords are on the outside of the circle and the minor chords are on the inside. Going clockwise, each chord is a 4th above the previous chord. Counterclockwise, each chord is a 5th above the previous one. Thus, going clockwise, D is a 4th above A; G is a 4th above D and so on. Moving counterclockwise, E is a 5th above A; B is a 5th above E and so on.

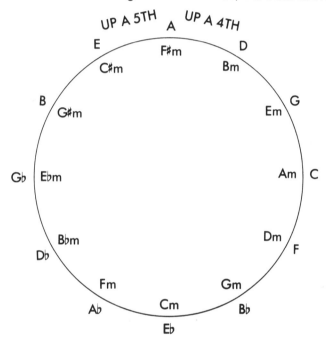

This diagram is useful because it puts each chord between its closest "relatives." For example, if a song is in the key of A, the D chord (a 4th higher) and the E (a 5th higher) are the chords most likely to be played. The 4 chord (D, in this case) is called the *subdominant*. The 5 chord (E) is in *dominant*. The 1 chord (A) is called the tonic. *This progression is called 1-4-5.*

RELATIVE MINORS

Every major chord has a "relative minor", a 3rd below the tonic (root). The relative minor of C is Am since A is a 3rd below C. On the circle of 5ths, the relative minors are written inside the circle next to their relative majors.

In any tune, the minor chords most likely to occur are the relative minors to the tonic, dominant (5 chord) and the sub-dominant (4 chord). For example, the minor chords that usually occur in the key of C are Am, Em and Dm (relative minors to 1, 5 and 4). When G is the key, Em, Am and Bm are likely to occur. They are the relative minors to G, C and D (1, 4, 5).

The relative minor is very similar to its relative major chord, and the two chords can often be interchanged in a progression without changing the overall sound. A C6 contains all the notes of its relative minor, Am (A, C, E). An Am7 contains all the notes of a C6 (C, E, G, A).

THE TONIC, SUBDOMINANT, DOMINANT (1-4-5) PROGRESSION

In a common progression, the chords move from the 1st to the 4th to the 5th.

In the key of G, the tonic chord is: the subdominant (4 chord):

and the dominant (5 chord), 2 frets above the subdominant:

Notice the relationship between the roots of 1-4-5 chords as they lie on the fingerboard:

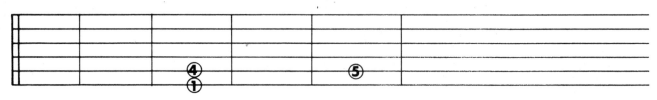

This 1-4-5 configuration holds true in all keys, anywhere on the fretboard:

| Tonic | Sub-dom. | Dom. | | Tonic | Sub-dom. | Dom. | | Tonic | Sub-dom. | Dom. |
| 1 | 4 | 5 | | 1 | 4 | 5 | | 1 | 4 | 5 |

Here is the same progression beginning with the C formation.

The tonic chord: The sub-dominant: And the dominant (2 frets higher):

The pattern of root notes on the fingerboard looks like this:

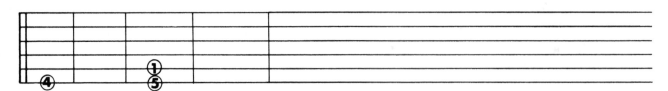

Apply this progression to other keys:

| 1 | 4 | 5 | | 1 | 4 | 5 | | 1 | 4 | 5 |

THE 2-5-1 PROGRESSION

It has been pointed out that the 1-4-5 chord group is like an immediate family, and that countless tunes use only these chords. The relative minors to 1, 4 and 5 are close relatives, often found in the company of the 1, 4 and 5 chords. Another close relative, found in many simple progressions, is the 2 chord. It lies two steps, counter-clockwise, from the tonic, on the circle of 5ths. (Thus, B is the 2 chord above A, E♭ is the 2 chord above D♭.)

Because it is a whole step above the tonic, the 2 chord is two frets above the 1 chord:

F
1 chord

G
2 chord

B♭
1 chord

C
2 chord

A chord progression often resolves to the tonic by going clockwise along the circle of 5ths, in a 2-5-1 sequence. Here are some examples of how the 2-5-1 progression appears in tunes. Even when the chords are altered (D9 instead of D), the 2-5-1 root relationship remains the same.

A7
2

D9
5

G7
1

Gm7
2

C7(♭9)
5

Fmaj7
1

D9
2

G7
5

C
1

E♭m9
2

A♭13
5

D♭maj9
1

B♭m9
2

E♭13
5

Ab6/9
1

F♯9
2

B7(♭9)
5

Emaj7
1

EXTENDED CIRCLE OF FIFTHS PROGRESSIONS

Often, the 2-5-1 progression is extended farther along the circle (counter-clockwise) to a 6-2-5-1 or 3-6-2-5-1 progression. For example, a common C progression is: A, D, G, C (6-2-5-1). A common G progression: Bm, E, Am, D, G (3-6-2-5-1). Many tunes move this way—clockwise along the circle of 5ths towards the one chord, or tonic. Stated another way, the chords move up a 4th until they resolve on the tonic.

Here is one way to play a clockwise circle of fifths progression, looking at the roots of the chords:

Each note is a 4th above the preceding note.   start here

Here are some chord progressions that move this way:

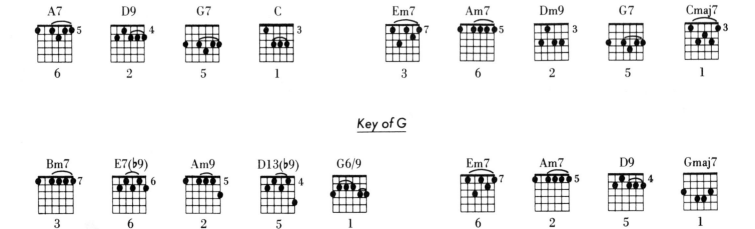

This type of chord movement is the basis for many jazz tunes—including some of the tunes in this book. Often it is used as a "turnaround" after a resolution to set up a repetition of the song.

SCALEWISE PROGRESSIONS

The tonic note of the starting chord follows the scale, up or down:

Scale Intervals

or

The 2nd and 3rd chords in the scale are usually minor chords; the 4th chord can be minor or major.

The chords may occur "out of order":

"Inbetween" chords may be added:

In these scalewise progressions, the "inbetween" chords are diminished chords. A tonic with the 3rd interval in the bass is substituted for the 3 chord.

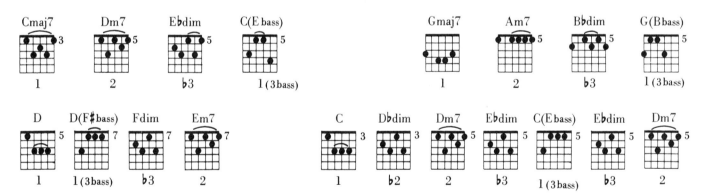

Wes Montgomery had a favorite minor chord ascending pattern related to the following scalewise movement:

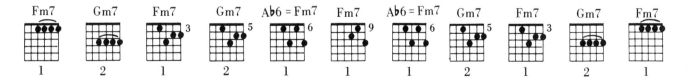

DESCENDING MINOR CHORD PROGRESSION

In this often-used pattern, the tonic note of a minor chord descends to form new chords. The sequence usually leads from a minor chord to the 4 chord of its relative major. For example, the Am eventually resolves to F. (F is the 4 chord to C. C is the relative major of Am.)

The descending note is circled.

With the descending note in the bass, this sequence results:

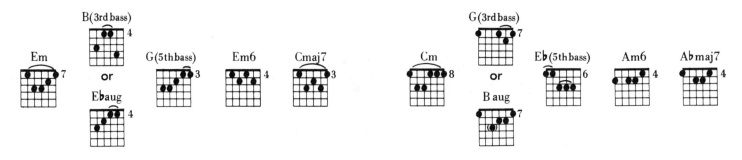

Note: see "EVERYTHING MUST CHANGE".

MINOR CHORD "TURNAROUND"

A turnaround is a brief musical phrase that concludes a longer passage—like a tag-ending. It has been noted that the 6-2-5-1 progression is a common turnaround.

Another popular turnaround includes a descending tone. In the key of C, as in the example below, the descending notes are C, B♭, A, A♭, G. When the 4 chord (F) becomes minor, it resolves to the tonic.

Note: see "CHEROKEE" and "YOU ARE SO BEAUTIFUL".

CHORD SUBSTITUTION (RULES FOR VARIATIONS OF CHORDS AND PROGRESSIONS)

The jazz soloist seldom plays a tune "straight"; he or she is always improvising, inventing, varying. One of the ways he or she does so is by altering the given chords and substituting new ones. The player who understands substitution rules cannot only vary a tune, he or she can better understand a more complicated chord progression. Many complex tunes boil down to basic progressions with substitutions added.

Though substituting a 6th, M7, etc. for a major chord depends upon personal taste and the context of a tune, here are the basic rules of chord embellishment:

DIRECT SUBSTITUTION (CHORD EMBELLISHMENT)

An A chord can be played: AM7, A6, A6/9, A add 9, AM9, A+, A♭5, Asus

An A7 chord can be played:
A9, A7+, A7♭5, A7♯9, A7♭9, A13, A13♭9, A7+5♯9, A7 sus, A11, A+11, A7+5♭9, A9+, A9♭5

An Am chord can be played: Am7, Am6, Am9, Am6/9, Am11, Am7♭5, Am/M7

In addition to embellishing a chord, the player can create a whole progression from a single chord. This is especially desirable when a tune hangs on one single chord, since it breaks up the monotony. For example, two measures of A can be played:

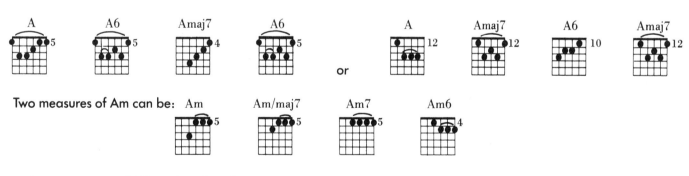

Two measures of Am can be:

and two measures of A7 can be played:

SCALEWISE SUBSTITUTION

Using the scalewise progression, noted in the last chapter, is another way to vary a passage that stays on one chord. Two measures of A can be played:

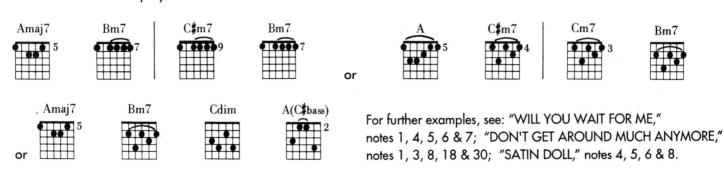

or

For further examples, see: "WILL YOU WAIT FOR ME," notes 1, 4, 5, 6 & 7; "DON'T GET AROUND MUCH ANYMORE," notes 1, 3, 8, 18 & 30; "SATIN DOLL," notes 4, 5, 6 & 8.

RELATIVE MAJOR AND MINOR SUBSTITUTION

The major chord and its relative minor can be interchanged.

This progression: C / / / | F / G / can be played: CM7 / Am7 / | Dm7 / G13 / or: C6 / Am / | Dm / Em /

See: "RENT TIMES," note 2.

DOMINANT MINOR SUBSTITUTION

Substitute the minor chord a fifth higher than the dominant 7th.

G7 / / / | C7 / F7 / can be played: Dm7 / G9 / | Gm7 C9 Cm9 F13

Here, the dominant minor substitution principle has been applied to each of the three chords in the progression. Dm7/G9 was substituted for G7, Gm7/C9 for C7, Cm9/F13 for F7.

The rule can be reversed, as well: Given a minor chord, substitute the dominant seventh type chord a 4th higher. Thus, this common "turnaround":
E E7 | A Am | E can be played: E E7 | A D9 | E Or, using the rule both ways: Bm7 E9 | A D9 | E

In the first instance, Am became D9 (the dom. 7th chord a 4th higher). In the second instance, the first measure changed as well—Bm7/E9 was substituted for E/E7. Here, the original dominant minor rule was used.

See: "BUSY SIGNAL," note 2; "MAKIN' WHOOPIE," notes 3, 4 & 10; "DON'T GET AROUND MUCH ANYMORE," notes 4, 7, 10 & 15.

CHORD SUBSTITUTIONS

Dominant 7th♭9 chords are almost exactly the same, note for note, as diminished chords a 5th higher.

C7(♭9) Gdim F7(♭9) Cdim

Is similar to   Is similar to

When a 7♭9 chord appears, a diminished chord a 5th higher can be substituted. G° can be substituted for C7♭9, D° for G7♭9, B♭° for E♭7♭9, etc.

The reverse is also true: Where a diminished chord appears, substitute a 7♭9 chord a 4th higher: C7♭9 for G°, G7♭9 for D°, etc..

Since diminished chords repeat every three frets, a 7♭9 chord can become any number of diminished chords. For example, this turnaround:

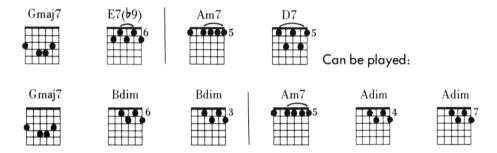

Gmaj7 E7(♭9) Am7 D7   Can be played:

Gmaj7 Bdim Bdim Am7 Adim Adim

B°, in two different positions, was substituted for E7♭9. D7 was played as A° since D7♭9 can be substituted for D7 (by the rule of direct substitution), and A° is a substitute for D7♭9. A°, then, is a substitute for a substitute! In general, where a dominant 7th chord appears, a diminished chord a 5th higher may be substituted.

See: "WILL YOU WAIT FOR ME," note 2; "MAKIN' WHOOPIE," note 11.

♭5 CHORD SUBSTITUTIONS

When any chord—especially a dom. 7th type—appears, substitute a chord a flatted fifth higher. For G, play a D♭; for C play a G♭. Once again, this rule is frequently applied to turnarounds. For example:

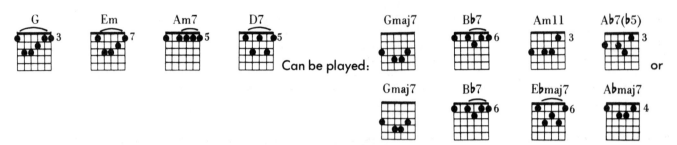

Here are some common variations of the 2-5-1 progression, using the ♭5 substitution principle:
This: Am   D7   G can be played: This: Dm   G7   C can be played:

See: "WILL YOU WAIT FOR ME," note 3; "RENT TIMES," note 3; "SATIN DOLL," note 7; "MAKIN' WHOOPIE," note 8; "DON'T GET AROUND MUCH ANYMORE," notes 11 & 21.

MINOR 6THS, 9THS, AND MINOR 7♭5 SUBSTITUTIONS

In the section on chord types, this formation was called by several names.

Cm7(♭5)   G♯9   E♭m6

Since each of these three chords contains the components of the other two, it stands to reason that *any* G♯9 formation can substitute for Cm7♭5...A number of other rules are apparent:

For a m6 chord substitute a m7♭5 chord a 6th higher. Substitute Cm7♭5 for E♭m6, Em7♭5 for Gm6, and so on.

Or, substitute a 9th chord, or any dom. 7th chord, a 4th higher. (See the "dominant minor substitution" principle.) Substitute G♯9 for E♭m6, C9 for Gm6, etc.

For a m7♭5 chord substitute a m6 chord a minor 3rd higher: E♭m6 for Cm7♭5, Cm6 for Am7♭5.

Or, move up a ♯5th and play a 9th or dom. 7th chord. Play G♯9 for Cm7♭5, D♯9 for Gm7♭5.

For a 9th chord substitute a m6 chord a 5th higher. (The "dominant minor substitution" principle again.) Substitute D♯m6 for G♯9, Gm6 for C9.

Or, move up a 3rd and play a m7♭5 chord. Play Cm7♭5 for G♯9, F♯m7♭5 for D9.

Depending on their context m6, m7♭5 and 9th chords often "exchange names." For example, this chord: may be called an Em7♭5, if it precedes an A chord: G m6

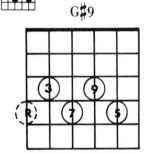

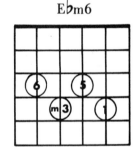

AUGMENTED SUBSTITUTIONS

Augmented chords are made up of ascending 3rds. Since every note is a 3rd higher than the last, the augmented chord repeats itself every four frets (just as the diminished chord, made of ascending ♭3rds, repeats every three frets).

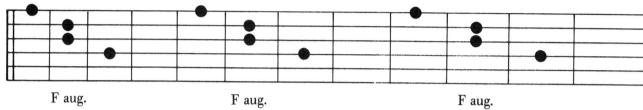

F aug.   F aug.   F aug.

As with diminished chords, every augmented chord can be named by any of its notes. For example: can be called F+ , C♯+ or A+ . All are interchangeable; each can be substituted for the others.

An augmented chord often leads to a chord that is a 4th higher. In a progression that moves from G to C, substitute G+ (by the direct substitution rule) for G. The G+ will tend to resolve on the 4 chord.

COMMON TONE SUBSTITUTION

Any substitution that sounds good is acceptable, whether or not any rule supports its. Often the original chord and its substitute share one common note, and that is the only connection between them. Very "open" or ambiguous sounding chords lend themselves to this kind of substitution. For instance, this turnaround:

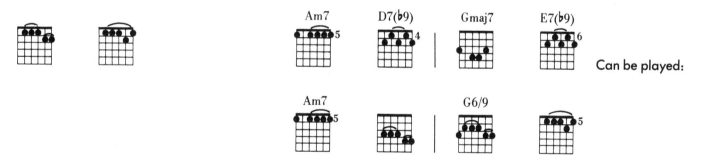

See: "WILL YOU WAIT FOR ME," Note 10, and "MAKIN' WHOOPIE," notes 9, 13, 18, 24 & 25.

ENDING (FALSE CADENCE) SUBSTITUTION

This ending device, often used in jazz improvisation, is called a "false cadence" in classical music. In a 2-5-1 progression, just before the song resolves, another 2-5 progression is inserted. The 2-5 insert begins a #5 higher than the original key.

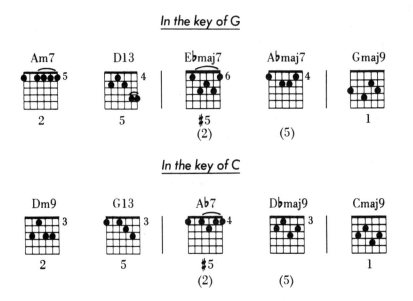

Ending chords common to jazz include the M7ths, M9ths, 6/9 chords, +11 chords, and, in a minor key, m6/9 chords.

For examples of the false cadence ending, see endings to "WILL YOU WAIT FOR ME," Note 9 and "YOU ARE SO BEAUTIFUL," Back-up Guitar Note 9.

CHORD SOLOING

A chord solo is a melody embellished with chords and rhythm. A good solo features a variety of chord voicings, interesting substitutions and improvisations that bridge gaps in the melody. *The highest note of a chord stands out.* This fact alone dictates many of the soloist's choices.

Since jazz expresses individual ideas and feelings, playing or memorizing the following solos is only a first step. The goal is improvisation. The solos do show, however, how to alter chords to suggest new melodies. This is an excellent way to approach improvisation for the first time.

The real purpose in practicing these solos—beyond adding good songs to one's repertoire—is to be able to create original chords solos. With this in mind, here is the best study program:

> 1) Listen to the chord solo on the cassette.
>
> 2) Strum along with the recording. Use the "SIMPLIFIED PROGRESSION" that precedes the actual transcription. Use any familiar voicing—the objective is to be comfortable with the progression.
>
> 3) Read "HIGHLIGHTS OF THE PROGRESSION". It explains chord movement throughout the song.
>
> 4) Play the solo, with and without the recording, as transcribed. Chord frames provide familiar formations and positions.
>
> 5) Read the "COMMENTARY AND NOTES" following the transcription. These notes explain why and how the substitutions and passing chords work. ("Direct substitutions" are not usually noted.)
>
> 6) A final suggestion: Transpose the tunes in this section, by ear, into several different keys. It's an excellent exercise for understanding chord relationships and an essential skill for the jazz guitarist.

SATIN DOLL

Words and Music by BILLY STRAYHORN,
DUKE ELLINGTON and JOHNNY MERCER

SIMPLIFIED PROGRESSION

Key of C ‖: Dm G7 |·/·| Em A7 |·/·| D7 | D♭7 | CM7 | ⌐1. A7 :‖ ⌐2. CM7 ‖

Bridge: | Gm C7 |·/· | FM7 |·/·| Am D7 |·/· | G7 |·/· ‖ repeat verse with 2nd ending

HIGHLIGHTS OF THE PROGRESSION

2-5-1 movement occurs throughout verse and bridge. In the verse, the 1 chord is not always played (Dm - G7, no C, and Em-A7, no D). It is played in the bridge (Gm-C7-F, and Am-D7-G7).

Parallel movement occurs in the verse and bridge; The Dm-G7 phrase is repeated a step higher (Em-A7); so is the Gm-C7 phrase (Am-D7).

♭5 substitution is "built into" the end of the verse (D7-D 7-CM7 instead of D7-G7-CM7).

Circle of fifths movement: The A7 at the end of the verse starts a 6-2-5-1 progression (A7-Dm-G7- implied C).

SATIN DOLL

By DUKE ELLINGTON, JOHNNY MERCER
and BILLY STRAYHORN

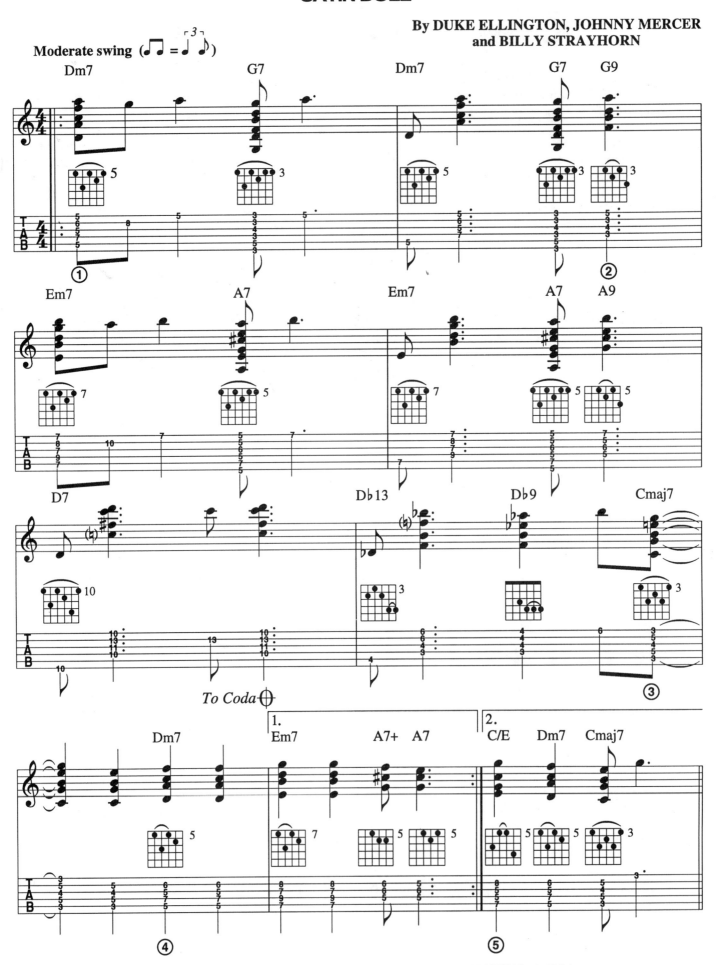

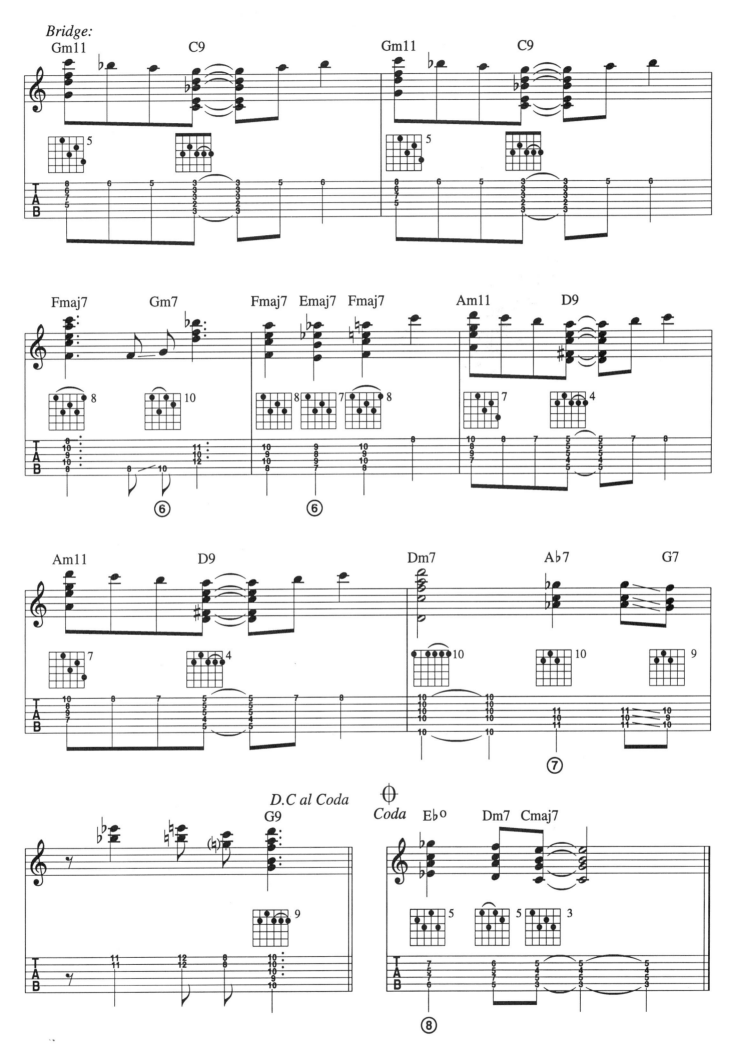

COMMENTARY AND NOTES

1) Dm7 is a direct substitution for Dm. The m7 chord is subtler than the minor chord.

2) G9 is another direct substitution (for G7). In this case, the melody note (A) dictates the substitution. Both types of direct substitution happen throughout the chord solos and they will not be noted hereafter.

3) In the SIMPLIFIED PROGRESSION, CM7 falls in the next measure. Here, the soloist plays it at the end of the previous measure because of a "rhythmic anticipation". Again, this happens too often to note.

4) Dm7 and Em7 (in the next bar) are scalewise "filling in". They are less static than playing two bars of CM7, and the Em7 chord sets up the A7 "turnaround" chord.

5) C/E and the next two chords complete another scalewise "fill-in" progression: C-Dm-C/E-Dm-C, all of which is a "second ending" for the eight-bar verse.

6) Gm7 is more scalewise fill-in. The EM7 is also fill-in. Along with the Gm7, it saves you from two static bars of F.

7) Ab7 is a b5 substitution for Dm7 and it sets up the G7 (which is the same chord as Ab7, one fret lower).

8) Eb° and Dm7 finish yet another scalewise fill-in (C-Dm-Eb°-Dm-C). These scalewise fillers could also be called turn-arounds, as they occur at the end of an eight bar passage and set up a repeat or lead to a bridge.

RENT TIMES
Music by FRED SOKOLOW

SIMPLIFIED PROGRESSION

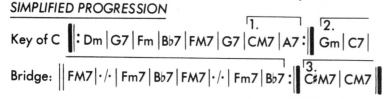

HIGHLIGHTS OF THE PROGRESSION

Parallel movement occurs when duplicate chord progressions in different keys appear in one song. In "RENT TIMES" parallel 2-5-1 movement occurs at the beginning of the verse: Dm-G7 is an incompleted 2-5-1 to C; Fm-Bb7 is a similar 2-5-1 to a new momentary key of Eb.

The m3rd jump (from the key center of C to Eb) is a typical way to change key centers.

The turnaround at the end of the verse—an A7 (the 6th to C)—sets up the 2-5 (Dm-G7) at the beginning of the verse.

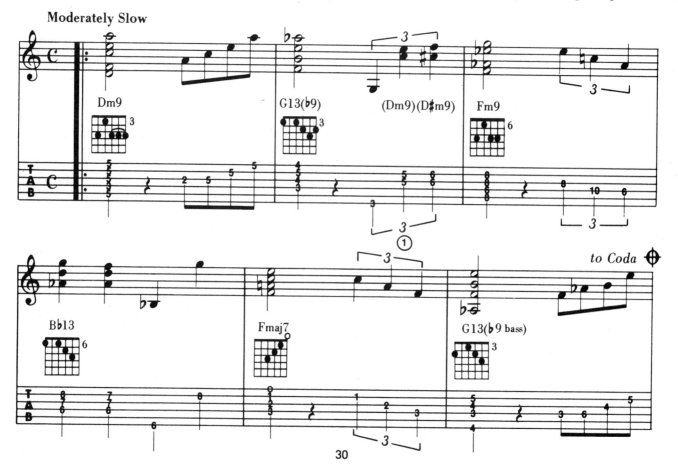

30

RENT TIMES

**Music by
FRED SOKOLOW**

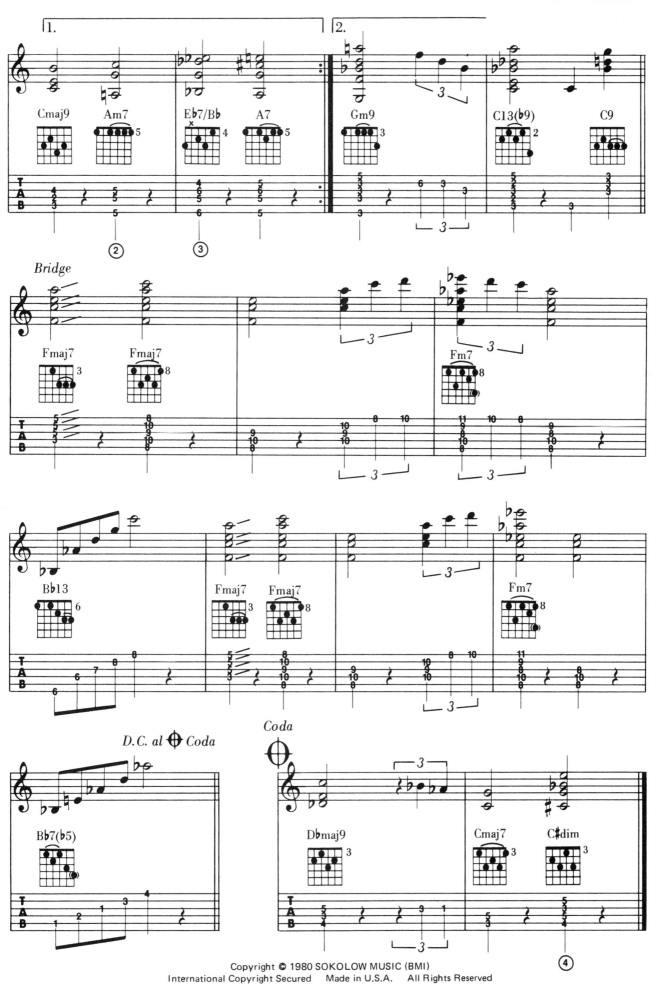

COMMENTARY AND NOTES

1) The Dm9 and D#m9 are passing chords that "walk up" to the Fm9. They are a variation of the usual scalewise movement.

2) Am7 is a relative minor substitute for C.

3) Eb7 is a b5 substitution for A7. The 5th in the bass (A#) "sets up" the A7 which is to follow.

4) The tune ends on CM7. The C#° sets up the Dm that will start the tune again. It creates a scalewise progression: C, C#°, Dm.

WILL YOU WAIT FOR ME
Music by FRED SOKOLOW

SIMPLIFIED PROGRESSION

Key of C ‖: FM7 Em | Eb° | Dm G | CM7 | Fm Bb | EbM7 Cm | Am D7 | G7 :‖ ⌐1. Am Dm G7 | CM7 ‖ ⌐2.

Bridge: ‖ Bm7b5 E7 | Am | Bm7b5 E7 | Am | Am7b5 D7 | Gm | Am7b5 D7 | G7 ‖ Repeat verse with 2nd ending.

HIGHLIGHTS OF THE PROGRESSION

<u>Scalewise movement</u> occurs at the beginning of the verse from FM7 down to CM7. (FM7-Em-Eb°-Dm-[G]-Cm7).

<u>2-5-1 movement</u> occurs throughout. (In the verse: Dm-G-C, Fm-Bb-EbM7 and elsewhere; in the chorus, Bm7b5-E7-Am and Am7b5-D7-Bm).

<u>6-2-5-1</u> (circle of fifths) occurs at the end of both the verse and bridge (since the bridge resolves to C).

<u>Parallel movement</u> occurs in the bridge: the first 4 measures (2-5-1, 2-5-1 in Am) are duplicated in the next 4 (2-5-1, 2-5-1 in G).

WILL YOU WAIT FOR ME

Music by
FRED SOKOLOW

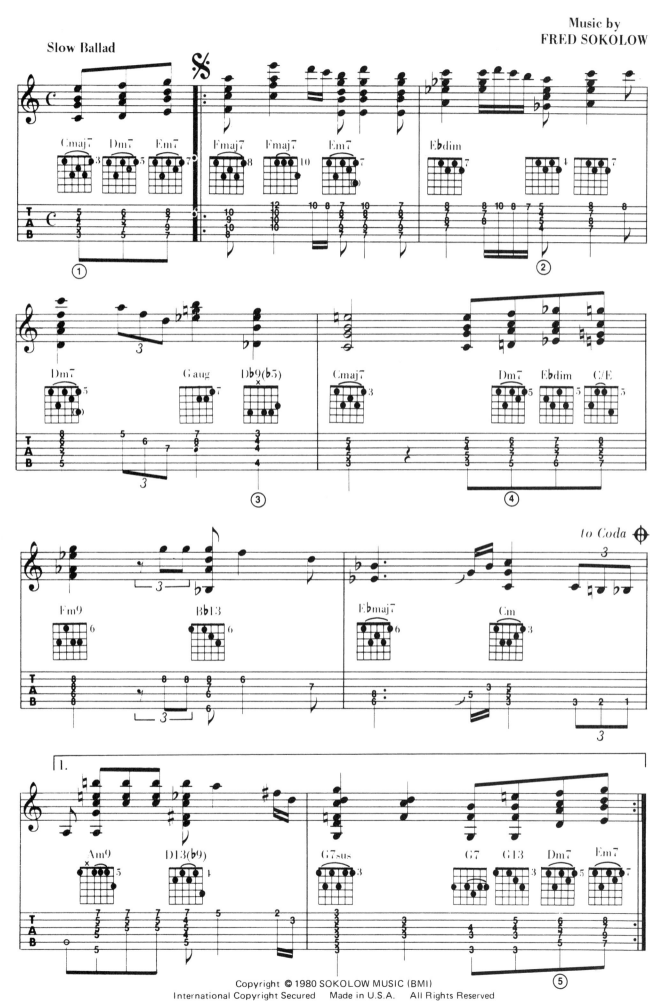

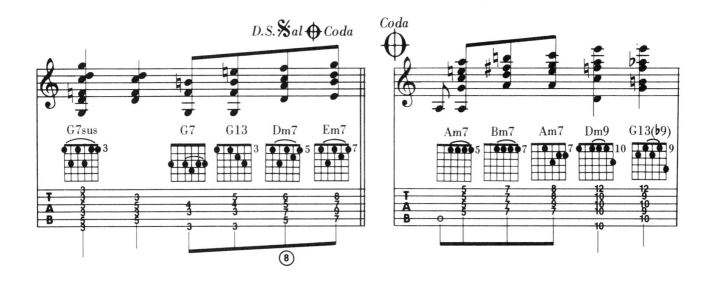

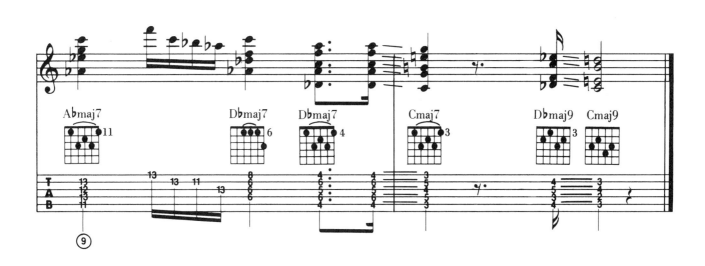

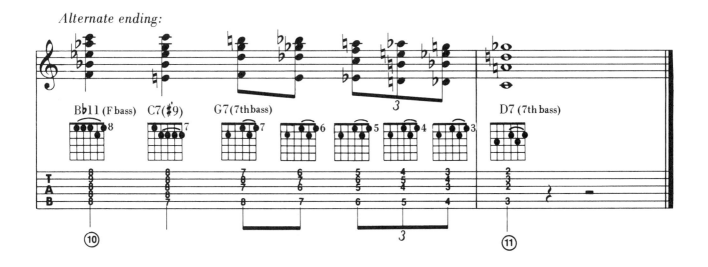

COMMENTARY AND NOTES ON CHORD SOLO

1) The "pickup notes" (the notes before the first full measure) are a typical scalewise progression from C (the tonic) to F.

2) Since the diminished chord repeats itself every three frets, the two chords used here are interchangeable.

3) Db9b5 is a b5 substitute for G. It is a common way to embellish a 5-1 phrase (from G to C, in this case).

4) Here is another typical scalewise progression from C to F: C, Dm, Eb°, C (E bass) F.

5) Except for the G chord, this is the same scalewise progression used for the "pickup" at the beginning of the tune.

6) Bm7 is a scalewise substitution for Am. It leads to a higher voicing of Am.

7) This Bm7b5 is also a Dm6 (see p. 24 on "m6ths, 9ths, and m7b5 chords.")

8) (See 5).

9) The CODA is a "false cadence" ending (see p. 26), beginning on the AbM7.

10) Here is an alternate way to end the tune using "common tone" substitutions. (See p. 25). C is the highest note in both Bb11 and C7#9.

11) D7 differs by only one note from C+11, a common ending chord for the key of C.

BUSY SIGNAL

Music by FRED SOKOLOW

SIMPLIFIED PROGRESSION

Key of G ‖: Am | D7 | GM7 | Bb7 | Am | D7 | GM7 | G7 | CM7 | Cm | Bm | Bb° | Am | D7 | GM7 Bb7 | EbM7 Ab7 :‖

HIGHLIGHTS OF THE PROGRESSION

<u>2-5-1 movement</u> dominates the tune (Am-D7-GM7)

<u>Scalewise movement</u> occurs in measures 9-13. These chords not only go down the scale by virtue of the descending bass line; but notes within the chords create downward scales, as well.

A common <u>turnaround</u> (G-Bb-Eb-Ab) occurs in the last two measures, leading to a repetition of the tune.

BUSY SIGNAL

Music by
FRED SOKOLOW

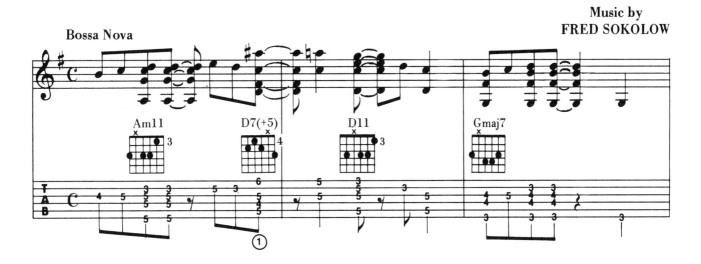

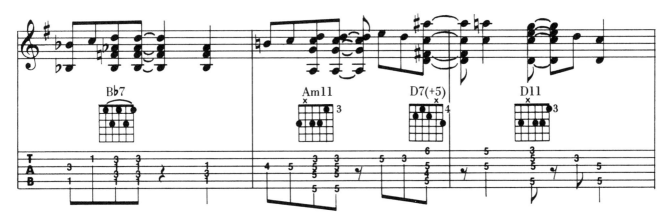

Improvisation

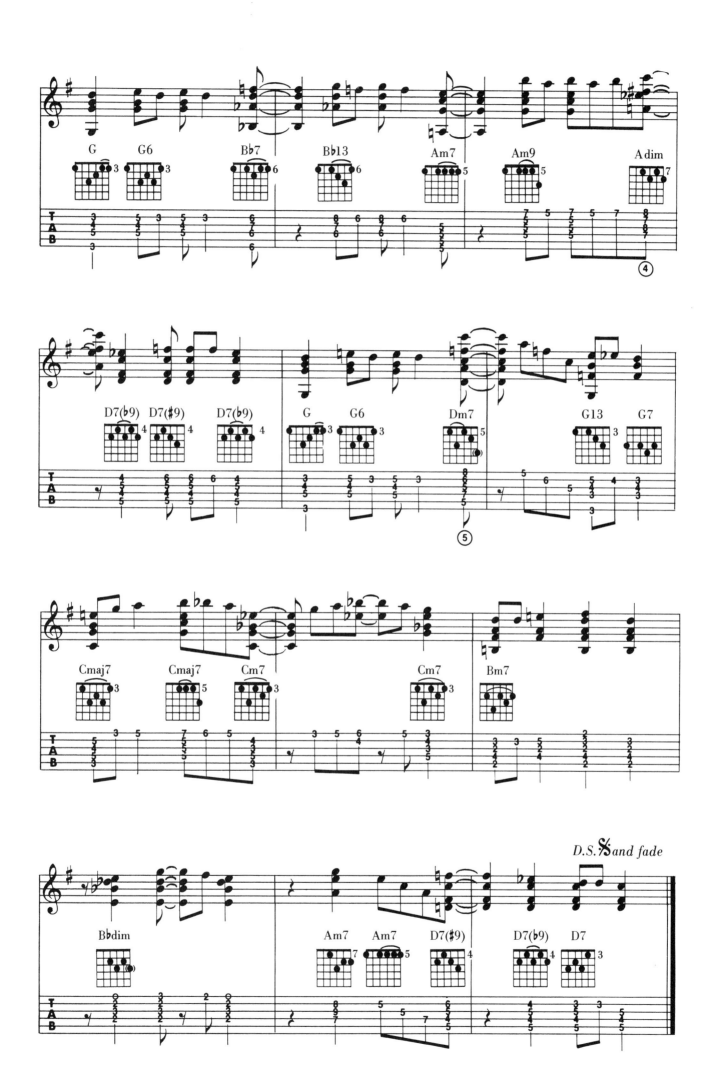

COMMENTARY AND NOTES

1) The D chord, which should fall in the 2nd measure, is played at the end of the 1st measure. This kind of rhythmic anticipation is typical to bossa nova tunes. It occurs throughout the solo.

2) Dm is a dominant minor substitution for G7.

3) The "D" note stays on top of the last four chords in the progression. IMPROVISATION—The soloist adds 6ths, 13ths, b9ths and #9ths, etc., to spark new melodic ideas.

4) A° is a substitute for D7b9, by the b9 substitution rule.

5) The same as 2).

MAKIN' WHOOPIE

Lyric by GUS KAHN
Music by WALTER DONALDSON

SIMPLIFIED PROGRESSION

Key of Eb ‖: Eb | Bb7 | Eb7 | Ab Abm | Eb | B7 Bb7 | Eb | B7 Bb7 :‖ [1.] | [2.] Eb ‖

Bridge: | G° | Fm | Abm | Eb | G° | Fm | Abm | Eb ‖ repeat verse with second ending.

HIGHLIGHTS OF THE PROGRESSION

1-4-5: Except for Abm (the minor 4 chord) and B7 (a b5 variation of the more typical 2 chord, or Fm) the eight-bar verse is all 1, 4, and 5. If you leave out the B7, the progression fits many other standards, such as "Ain't Misbehavin'", "The Glory of Love" and "Tiptoe Through the Tulips". Play the first eight bars and hum these tunes.

From the Broadway Musical Produciton "WHOOPEE!"
MAKIN' WHOOPEE!

By GUS KAHN and
WALTER DONALDSON

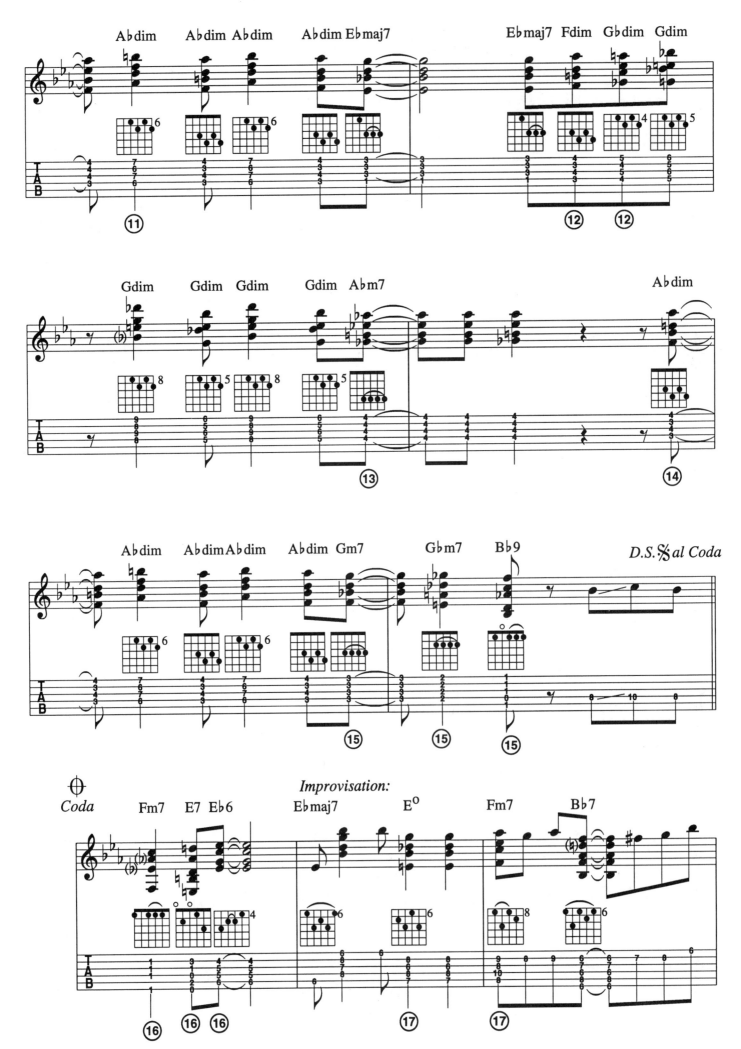

1) E° and Fm7 are part of a scalewise progression that starts with E♭. The four-chord phrase (E♭-E°-Fm7-B♭7) is also a popular intro or vamp, used in countless standards.

2) B7 is a passing chord that leads to B♭7.

3) B♭m7 is a dominant minor substitution for E♭7.

4) D♭9 is a reverse dominant minor substitution for A♭m.

5) Gm7 and Cm7 are part of a "cycling back" on a circle of fifths. The progression is Gm7-Cm7-Fm-B♭7-E♭ which is 3-6-2-5-1 in the key of E♭. The B9, which is written into the tune, takes the place of Fm in this chord series, as it's a ♭5 substitute.

6) D is a passing chord that leads to E♭.

7) G♭m7 is a passing chord leading to Gm7. Gm7 begins a cycling back (3-6-2-5-1) as in note #5, above. The second G♭m7 is a ♭5 substitute for C7. The Fm7 in the second ending is the 2 chord in the cycle.

8) E is a ♭5 substitute for B♭7 in the above-mentioned cycle (#7).

9) B♭m7 is a common tone substitution for G°.

10) D♭9 is a dominant minor reverse substitute for A♭m.

11) The diminished chords in this bar are ♭9 substitutes for D♭9 (see #10 for an explanation of the use of D♭9, and see page 23 on ♭9 substitutes).

12) F° and G° are passing chords that lead to G.

13) As in note #9, A♭m7 is a common tone substitute for Fm.

14) Same as #11.

15) Gm7 and the next few chords are a cycling back, as in note #7.

16) The same as the 2nd ending.

17) Same as #1.

18) A7♭5 is a ♭5 substitute for E♭7. Note that E♭7, A7♭5 and A♭maj7 all have a common tone: their highest note is E♭.

19) Same as #4.

20) Same as #5.

21) Gm7 begins a 3-6-2-5-1 cycle (Gm-C7-Fm-B♭7).

22) E7♯9 is a ♭5 substitute for B♭7 in the above-mentioned cycle.

23) This eight-bar section starts with the same substitutes as the first improvised eight-bars, but the melody and rhythm are completely different.

24) The next four bars are made up of chords whose highest note is E. During this long, common-tone progression, the chords descend in a chromatic (one fret at a time) movement to the tonic: A7-A♭-E♭/G-G-F7-E-E♭.

25) G♭6 is a common tone substitute for E♭.

26) This bar is very similar to the second ending (notes #7, #8 and #9).

DON'T GET AROUND MUCH ANYMORE

Words by BOB RUSSELL
Music by DUKE ELLINGTON

SIMPLIFIED PROGRESSION

Key of B♭ (F7) ‖: B♭ |·/· | G7 |·/· | C7 | F7 | B♭ | F7 :‖ [1.] [2. B♭ |·/· ‖]

Bridge: E♭ | E♭m | B♭ |·/· | C7 |·/· | F7 |·/· ‖ Repeat verse with second ending.

HIGHLIGHTS OF THE PROGRESSION:

The first eight bars is a circle of fifths: 1-6-2-5-1.

The bridge starts with 4-4 minor-1, a typical bluesy progression. It ends with a 2-5-1 (C7-F7-leading to B in the repeat of the first eight bars).

DON'T GET AROUND MUCH ANYMORE

By DUKE ELLINGTON
and BOB RUSSELL

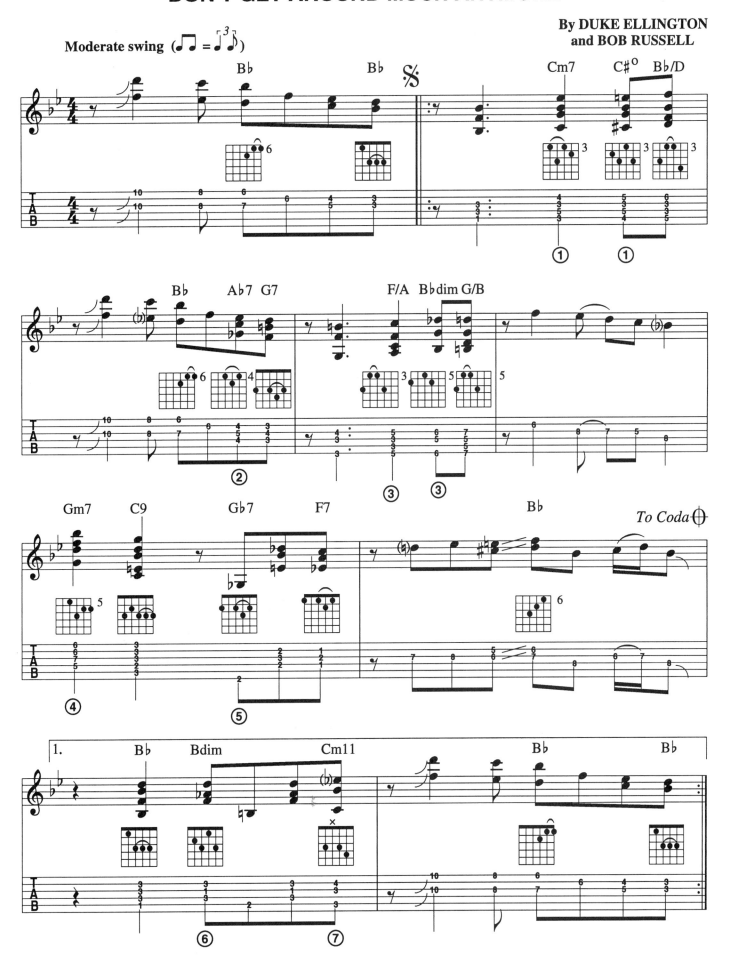

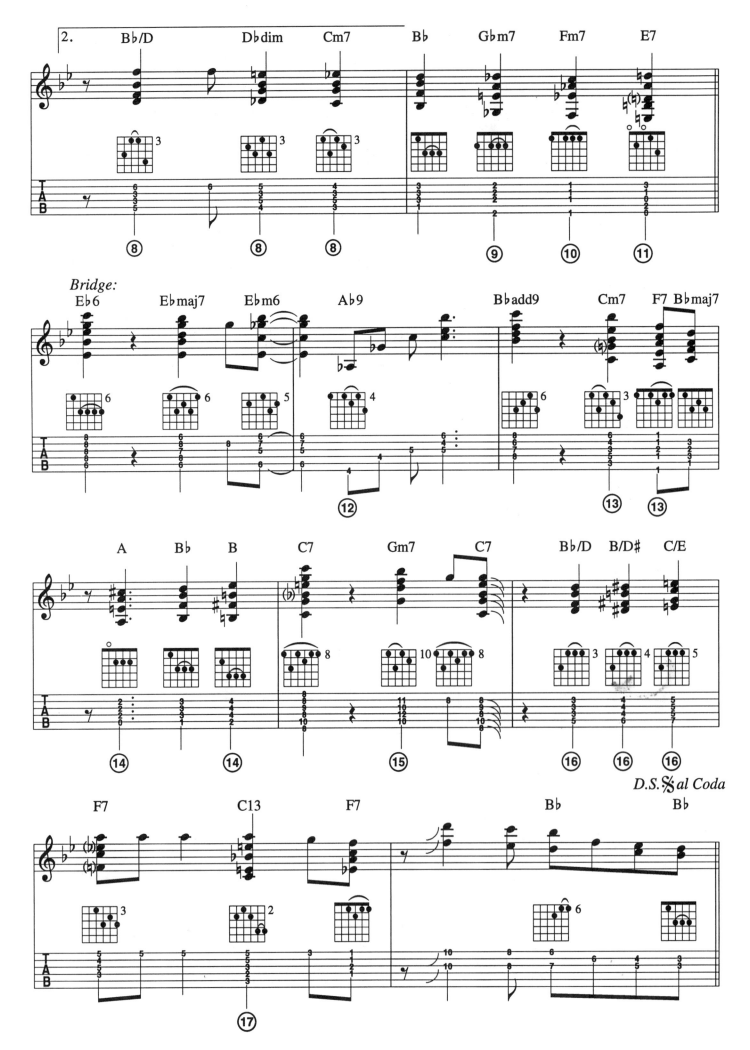

47

COMMENTARY AND NOTES

1) Cm7, C#° and B♭/D are a scalewise progression that stays in B♭ (it doesn't lead to another chord).

2) A♭7 is a passing chord leading to G7.

3) F/A, B♭° and G/B make up a scalewise G progression.

4) Gm7 is a dominant minor substitute for C9.

5) G♭7 is a passing chord that leads to F7.

6) B° leads, scalewise, from B♭ to Cm11.

7) Cm11 is a dominant minor substitute for F7.

8) B♭/D, D♭° and Cm7 are part of a B♭ scalewise progression that remains in B♭.

9) G♭m7 is an "approach chord" (passing chord) to Fm7. Along with Fm7 and E7, it is a scalewise progression leading to E♭.

10) Fm7 is a dominant minor substitute for B♭7. Also, see the previous note (#9).

11) E7 is a ♭5 substitute for B♭. Also, see note #9.

12) A♭9 is a reverse dominant minor substitute for E♭m.

13) Cm7 and F7 "cycle back" and add a 2-5-1 progression to the two bars of B♭.

14) A and B are both "approach chords" that create a chromatic move from B♭ to C7.

15) Gm7 is a dominant minor substitute for C7.

16) B♭/D, B/D# and C/E are part of a scalewise move from C7 to F7.

17) C13 "cycles back" a step, making 5-1 (F7-B♭) into 2-5-1.

IMPROVISATION

18) B°, Cm7, C#° and B♭/D make up a scalewise progression that remains in B♭, similar to the progression in note #1.

19) A6 is a passing chord. You can add variety to a bar or two with no chord changes by moving the original chord up or down a fret, then back.

20) Dm7 is a dominant minor substitute for G7.

21) D♭7♭5 is a ♭5 substitute for G7 (or for G9+).

22) B13 is a passing chord, as in note #19.

23) Cm9 is a dominant minor substitute for F9.

24) D♭°, along with the previous chord and the chord that follows, makes a scalewise progression from B to Cm (B♭/D-D♭°-Cm7).

25) Cm7 is a dominant minor substitute for F9. Notice how this and the previous bar quote the song "New York, New York".

26) A9 and A♭9 are part of chromatic descending progression from B♭9 to G9.

27) B7 is an approach chord to C7.

28) Gm7 is a dominant minor substitute for C7.

29) Cm9 is a dominant minor substitute for F9. Notice how this bar and the previous one quote another Ellington tune, "I'm Beginning To See The Light".

30) B♭/D starts another downward scalewise progression that remains in B♭, similar to # 8.

 # SINGLE NOTE SOLOING

Improvisation—the pure invention of melody—is an art that is developed through years of playing. The jazz guitarist thinks like a composer; he or she invents new melodies to fit a given chord progression.

Scales are the basis for single note soloing. There are a variety of scales that agree harmonically with a given chord or progression. The goal is to master these scales and their relationships to chords. A good working knowledge of the fretboard will naturally follow. Together, these two abilities will enable the guitarist to create unique melodies based on personal ideas and feelings. That is true improvisation!

The scales in this chapter offer a basis for improvising as well as a way to become familiar with the fretboard. Learn each scale—how to play it, and how to use it in a progression. Then practice the scales while playing along with records, with other players, and with the recording in this book.

 # KEY CENTERS

Although a soloist must _know_ the chord progression in the tune he plays, he or she does not have to _play_ a different scale for each chord change. By observing "key centers" the soloist can play one scale through many chord changes.

Music constantly sets up tension and resolves it. Most tunes ultimately resolve on the tonic chord, but there may be many key changes and temporary resolutions along the way. A soloist can regard each of these resolutions as a key center. He or she can choose which scales to play according to which key centers he or she perceives in the tune.

Refer to the simplified progression for "SATIN DOLL." Although the tune is in the key of C, the first four bars of the bridge come to rest on F; in fact, the first half of the bridge is a 2-5-1 to F. A soloist could play notes within an F major scale during these bars. Similarly, the next four bars are in the key of G (Am -D7-G is a 2-5-1 to G). The soloist could switch to the G major scale during these bars. So, the key center for the first half of the bridge is F, and the key center for the second half is G.

Key centers present many possibilities to the soloist. In a 2-5-1 progression, the "1" chord is the key center. The soloist can play the major scale of this tonic chord throughout the progression. To create a "blues" effect, he or she can play a blues scale, in the same key. Or, to create a feeling of movement, he or she can change scales with each chord change. All these possibilities, and many more, will be covered.

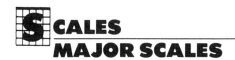

SCALES
MAJOR SCALES

Here is a G major scale. Its starting note is the G on the 6th string. Like all the scales in this section, it is moveable. Start it two frets higher and it becomes an A major scale. Practice the G scale and G scale exercise forwards and backwards (ascending and descending), and do likewise with the exercises that accompany it. *(The starting note, or root, of each scale diagram is circled.)*

G Major Scale

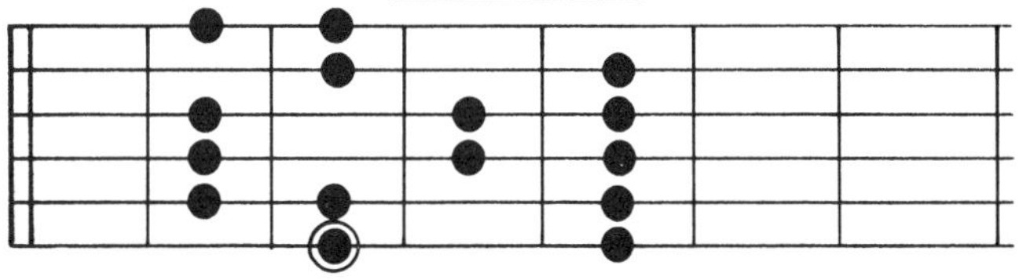

G Major Scale

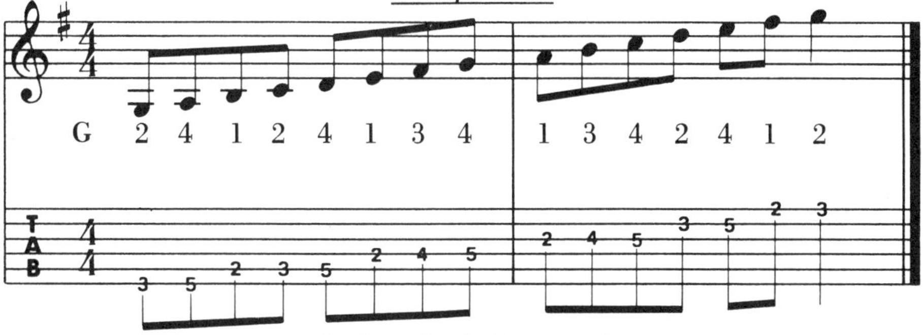

G Major Scale Exercise (A)

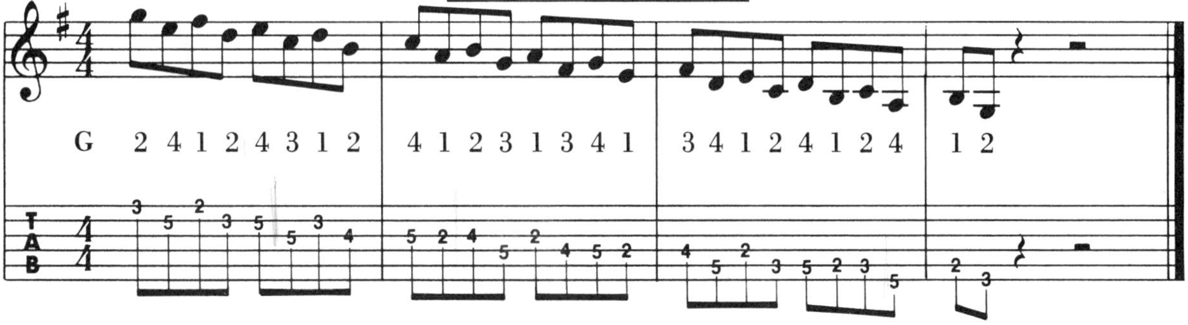

G Major Scale Exercise (B)

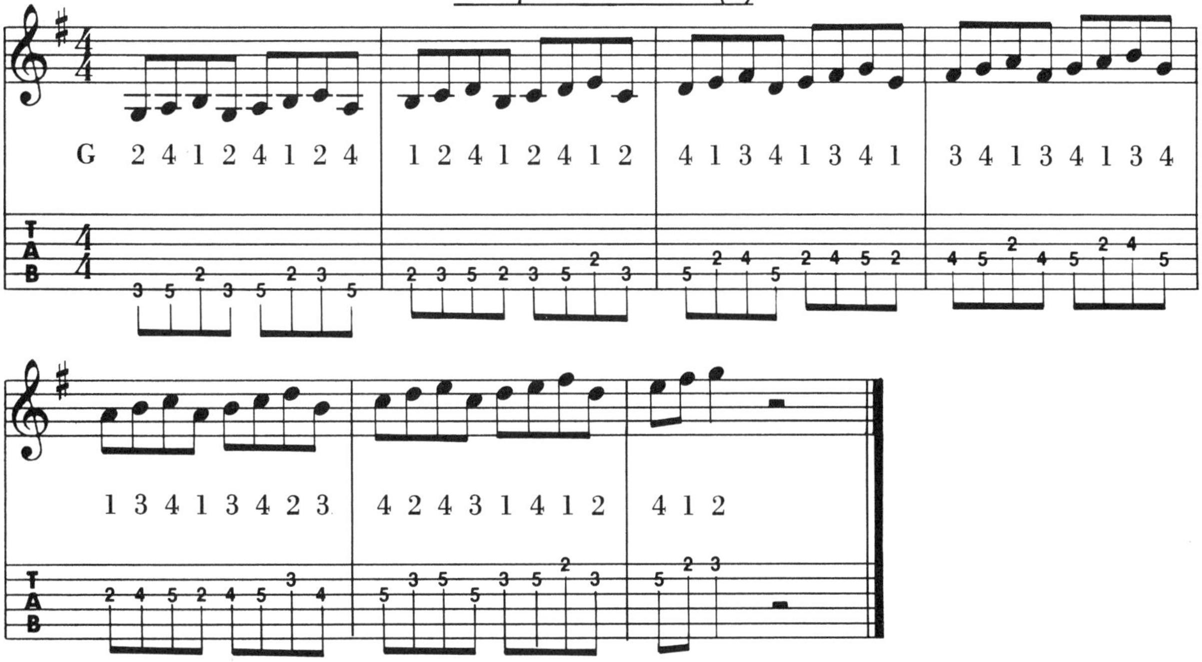

Here are two ways to play a D major scale. Both start with the root note on the 5th string, and both are moveable—two frets higher they become E major scales. Once again, practice ascending and descending, and do the same with the exercises that accompany them.

D Major Scale

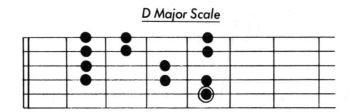

D Major Scale

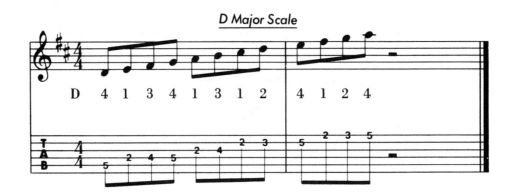

D   4   1   3   4   1   3   1   2 | 4   1   2   4

D Major Scale Exercise (A)

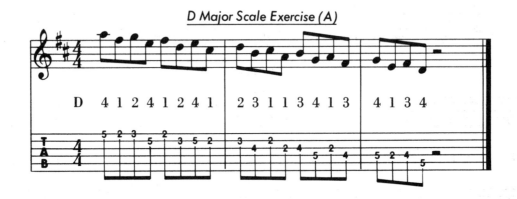

D   4 1 2 4 1 2 4 1 | 2 3 1 1 3 4 1 3 | 4 1 3 4

D Major Scale Exercise (B)

D   4 1 3 4 1 3 4 1 | 3 4 1 3 4 1 3 4 | 1 3 1 1 3 1 2 3 | 1 2 4 1 2 4 1 2 | 4 1 2 4 1 2 4

D Major Scale (Alternate Fingering)

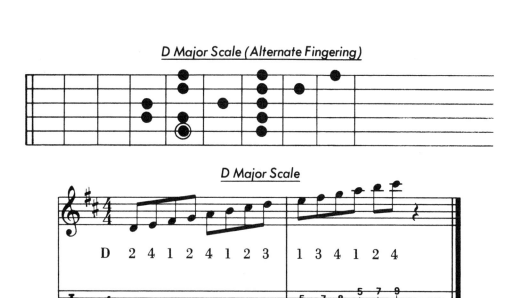

D Major Scale

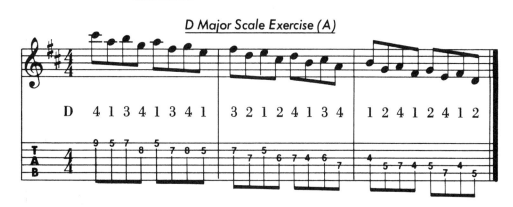

D 2 4 1 2 4 1 2 3 1 3 4 1 2 4

D Major Scale Exercise (A)

D 4 1 3 4 1 3 4 1 3 2 1 2 4 1 3 4 1 2 4 1 2 4 1 2

D Major Scale Exercise (B)

D 2 4 1 2 4 1 2 4 1 2 4 1 2 4 1 2 4 1 3 4 1 3 4 1 3 4 2 3 4 2 4 3

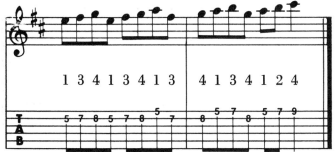

1 3 4 1 3 4 1 3 4 1 3 4 1 2 4

A major scale can often be played through a long chord sequence. For example, G is the key center in Scale Exercise #1, a circle of 5ths progression. The soloist plays G scales throughout the chord sequence.

SCALE EXERCISE #1

Play Scale Exercise #1 with the recording. Then turn off the lead track and improvise with the accompaniment, using the G major scale. The same progression is repeated many times in a row. Keep practicing the G major scale throughout these repeats.

SCALE EXERCISE #2

In this exercise the soloist divides the chord sequence into two key centers: A and G. Bm7 and E9, in the first two measures, are considered the 2 and 5 to the key of A. Thus, A major scales are played during these measures. Similarly, Am7 and D7♭9, in the next two measures, are thought of as 2 and 5 to the GM7 chord. Therefore, G major scales are played during these measures.

Follow the same practice procedure as in Scale Exercise #1: learn this brief solo as written, then improvise with the accompaniment track, using the new key centers as a basis for soloing.

Improvisation need not be limited to the notes within the G scale. The scale is only a point of departure. For instance, when a G major scale is played over a G9 chord, the dominant 7th, which is part of a G9 chord, may sound better than the major 7th. Any scale can be altered in this manner to fit any chord.

 **LUES SCALES**

These pentatonic (five-note) scales achieve a "blues" sound by including the ♭3 and the dominant 7th intervals.

G Blues Scale
6th String Root

G Blues Scale

G   1 4 1 3 1 3 1 3   │   1 4 1 4

Relate the left-hand
fingering position
to this chord:

Gm

C Blues Scale
5th String Root

C Blues Scale

C   1 4 1 3 1 3 2 4   │   1 4

Relate the left-hand
fingering position
to this chord:

Cm

In the next exercise, the soloist uses a G blues scale throughout this circle of 5ths progression, consider the entire passage as having a G key center. Notice how the sound of the blues scale differs from the major scale solo.

SCALE EXERCISE #3

Bm7   E9   Am7   D7(♭9)   Gmaj7

G ├──────────────── G blues ────────────────┤

The blues sound is a very important element in jazz music. For more information about blues scales, positions and licks, see my Almo Publication, BASIC BLUES FOR GUITAR.

PENTATONIC SLIDING SCALES

These pentatonic scales have a "major", rather than "blues" sound. They "slide" into different positions up and down the fretboard.

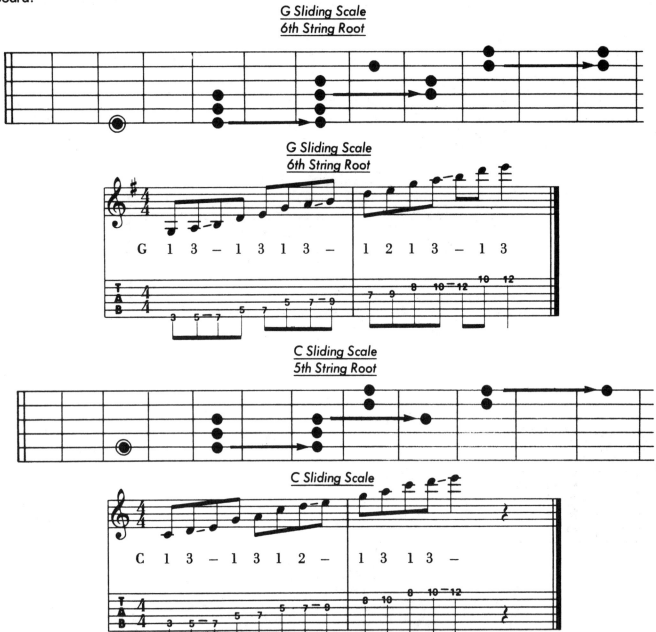

The pentatonic sliding scales fit wherever a major scale fits, and can often take the place of a blues scale. In Scale Exercise #4 the "turnaround" progression is divided into two key centers—E and G. An E sliding scale is played in the Bm-E (5-1) section, and a G sliding scale in the Am-D-G (2-5-1) section. A G sliding scale could have been played throughout the passage.

SCALE EXERCISE #4

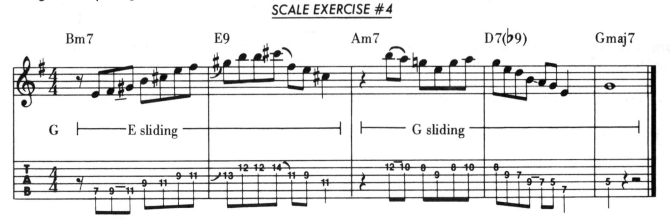

 **INOR SCALES**

Though the blues scale can be played with a minor chord (G blues with a Gm chord, for example), the "natural minor" scale contains more notes and conveys the minor sound more completely.

<u>G "Natural Minor" Scale (Bb Major)</u>
<u>6th String Root</u>

The left-hand finger position resembles the Gm chord:

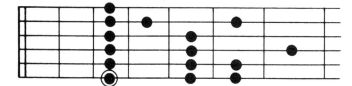

G "Natural Minor" Scale

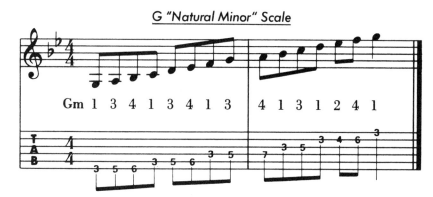

<u>C "Natural Minor" Scale (Eb Major)</u>
<u>5th String Root</u>

The left-hand finger position resembles the Cm chord:

C "Natural Minor" Scale

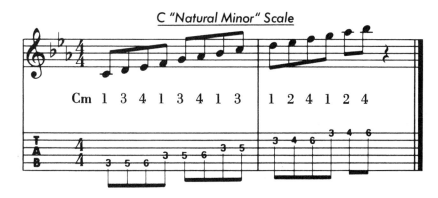

The notes in the natural minor scale duplicate the notes in the relative major scale. Thus Cm= Eb, Gm= Bb. (See the Circle of 5ths.)

The minor scale is used when the tone center is minor.

DIMINISHED SCALES

Diminished scales, like diminished chords, are made up of ascending minor 3rds. Any note in the scale can be considered the root.

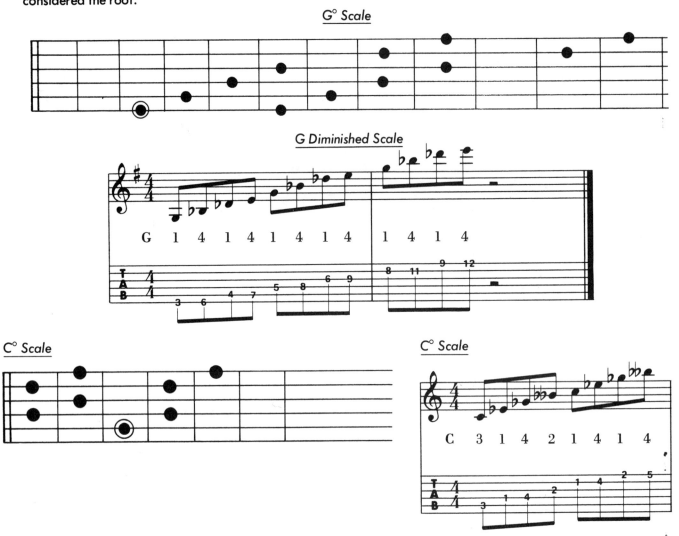

Scale Exercise #5 uses both the natural minor scales and diminished scales. A different scale is played for each chord change. Both dominant 7th chords (E9 and D7♭9) are treated like diminished chords, in keeping with the ♭9 substitution rule.

SCALE EXERCISE #5

 AUGMENTED SCALES

Augmented scales are made up of ascending whole tones—that is, each note is two frets (a whole step) higher than the last. Thus, any note in the scale can be considered the root note.

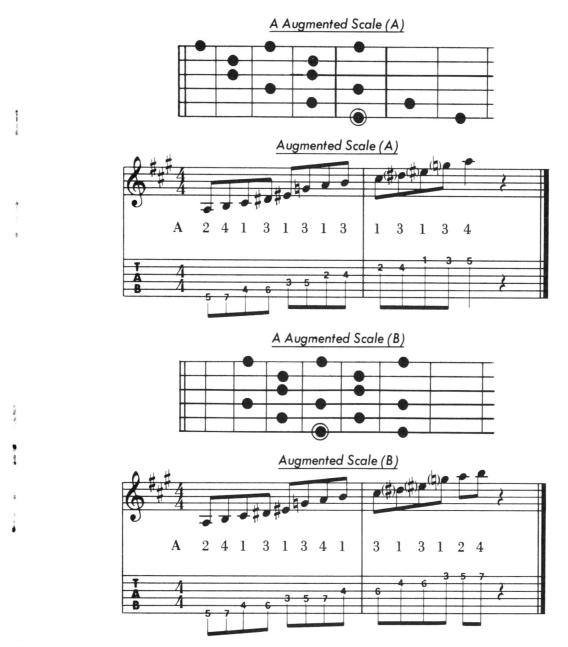

A Augmented Scale (A)

Augmented Scale (A)

A 2 4 1 3 1 3 1 3   1 3 1 3 4

A Augmented Scale (B)

Augmented Scale (B)

A 2 4 1 3 1 3 4 1   3 1 3 1 2 4

The augmented scale can be used with an augmented chord or a b5 chord. In Scale Exercise #6, the soloist plays E+ scales for the E9 chord and D+ scales for the D7b9, using the b9 substitution rule.

SCALE EXERCISE #6

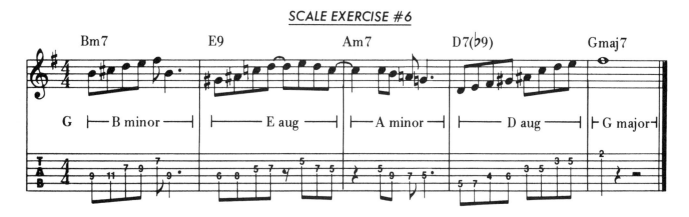

| Bm7 | E9 | Am7 | D7(b9) | Gmaj7 |

G ⊢— B minor —⊣ ⊢——— E aug ———⊣ ⊢— A minor —⊣ ⊢——— D aug ———⊣ ⊢ G major ⊣

SCALES AND CHORD FRAGMENTS

Sometimes a soloist will emphasize the feeling of chord movement in a rapid progression by playing a different scale for each chord. In this situation, it is helpful to know some "mini-scales" that are associated with "mini-chords," or "chord fragments." Scale Exercise #7 applies the chords and scale fragments shown below.

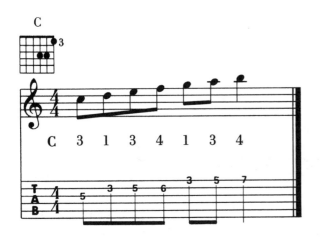

SCALE EXERCISE #7

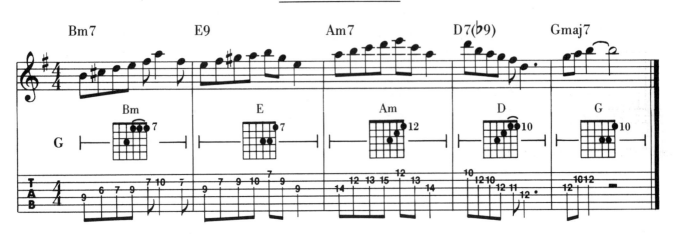

CALE SUBSTITUTION

Chord Substitution principles apply to scales as well. For example, an Am scale can be played with a C chord, because of the "relative minor" substitution rule. In Scale Exercise #5, the soloist applies the ♭9 substitution rule, and its corollary: where a dominant 7th chord occurs, substitute a diminished chord a 5th higher.

(See "CHARLIE'S BLUES" for more examples of diminished scale substitutions.)

Here are some other scale substitution ideas:

UGMENTED SCALE SUBSTITUTION

The augmented scale can be used with a ♭5 chord, or where a ♭5 chord can be substituted. In the progression: Am11 / A♭7♭5 / G, an A♭ augmented scale can be used with the A♭7♭5 chord, as stated in the rule above. In this example: Am11 / D9 / G, the A♭+ scale can be played with the D9, since A♭7♭5 can be substituted for the D9. (Note: the D+ scale, which contains the same notes as the A♭+ scale, can also be used.)

Augmented scales, like augmented chords, frequently resolve a 4th higher. A G+ scale, for instance, resolves to a C.

See: "CHEROKEE," Scale Note 3; "CHARLIE'S BLUES," Scale Note 1; "YOU ARE SO BEAUTIFUL," Scale Note 1; "EVERYTHING MUST CHANGE," Scale Note 1.

"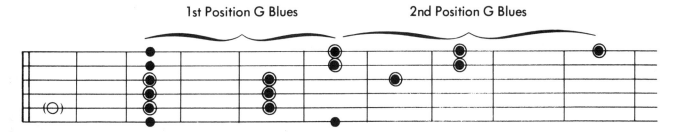ELATIVE MAJOR" SLIDING SCALE SUBSTITUTION

To get a "blues" sound, play a sliding pentatonic scale a minor 3rd above the actual key. This is the same as considering the original key to be minor, and playing the relative minor sliding scale. For example, in the key of G, play a B♭ sliding scale to effect a blues sound; B♭ is a ♭3rd above G, and is the relative major to Gm.

The notes of the B♭ sliding scale duplicate the notes of the G blues positions. (In the G blues scale diagram below, the B♭ sliding scale notes are circled.)

1st Position G Blues   2nd Position G Blues

See: "WILLOW WEEP FOR ME," Scale Note 2.

 # RELATIVE MINOR BLUES SCALE SUBSTITUTION

The relative minor blues scale can be played with any major chord. For example, play the A blues scale over a C chord (Am is the relative minor to C). The notes that result from this substitution duplicate the notes of the sliding scale in the original key. (The C sliding scale contains the same notes as the A blues scale.)

See: "YOU ARE SO BEAUTIFUL," Scale Note 5.

 # MAJOR 9TH CHORD SUBSTITUTION

When a major 9th or major 7th chord appears, play a major scale a 5th higher. Example: for GM9 (or GM7) play a D major scale.

See: "CHEROKEE," Scale Note 8; "YOU ARE SO BEAUTIFUL," Scale Notes 2 & 5.

 # 11TH CHORD SUBSTITUTION

When an 11th chord appears, play a major scale a whole step *down*. Example: for C11, play B♭ major scales.

See: "WE'VE ONLY JUST BEGUN," Scale Note 5.

 # +11TH CHORD SUBSTITUTION

When a +11 chord appears, play major scale a whole step *up*. Example: for G+11, play A major scales.

See: "WILLOW WEEP FOR ME," Scale Note 5.

 # HALF-DIMINISHED (m7♭5) CHORD SUBSTITUTION

Where a m7♭5 chord appears, play major scales a ♭5th higher. This rule is derived from the ♭5 rule of chord substitution. Example: for Em7♭5, play a B♭ major scale.

The m7♭5 chord often resolves "up a 4th." For example, Cm7♭5 often leads to an F chord. Following the half-diminished scale substitution rule, play a major scale one fret (one half-note) above the resolving chord (the 4 chord). For example: in a Cm7♭5-F7 progression, play an F♯ major scale for Cm7♭5, and an F scale for the F7.

See: "WILLOW WEEP," Scale Note 4; "YOU ARE SO BEAUTIFUL," Scale Note 3.

 # DOMINANT MINOR SUBSTITUTION

When a minor chord appears, play the minor scale a 5th higher. Example: for Gm7, play a Dm scale.

See: "YOU ARE SO BEAUTIFUL," Scale Note 4; "WE'VE ONLY JUST BEGUN," Scale Notes 1 & 3.

The solos that follow contain examples of all the substitution rules. But remember, as in chord substitution, the soloist relies on personal taste, as well as theoretical rules, when selecting which scales to play.

SINGLE NOTE SOLOS
HOW TO STUDY THE SINGLE NOTE SOLOS

Although it can be helpful to copy another player's "licks", it is not necessary to learn these solos exactly as recorded on the cassette. The main purpose of the transcriptions is to show how a soloist used key centers and scales to improvise. Making up similar solos using the ideas discussed in the last two chapters is the final objective.

Here is the best procedure to follow:

> 1) Listen to the solo on the recording.

> 2) Become familiar with the progression by playing back-up chords with the cassette. Use the simplified progression that precedes the transcription. Read "HIGHLIGHTS OF THE PROGRESSION."

> 3) Read "HOW THE SOLOIST IS THINKING." It explains how the soloist selected scales and divided the tune into key centers.

> 4) Copy the solo and play it with the recording. Use the transcription when necessary.

> 5) Tune out the lead track and solo over the accompaniment track on the cassette. Invent new solos, using the same guidelines as in the transcribed solo.

> 6) Make up different solo guidelines (key centers, scale substitutions) using the theories in the last two chapters. Improvise within those guidelines, using the accompaniment track as a backup.

Note—Listen to the (backup) rhythm guitar on the recording and try to imitate it. Notes will be provided with each tune explaining what techniques and styles the rhythm guitarist uses.

CHEROKEE
Written and Composed by RAY NOBLE

HIGHLIGHTS OF THE PROGRESSION

1-4-4m-1, the common blues turnaround, comprises the first part of the verse.

Circle of fifths movement occurs in the verse (G7, Cm, F7, leading back to Bb) and in the bridge. In fact, the bridge is one long circle of fifths back to Bb from C#.

Parallel movement: The bridge is divided into parallel 4-measure sections: 2/5/1/1 (key of B), 2/5/1/1 (A), 2/5/1/1 (G), 2/5/1/1 (F).

HOW THE SOLOIST IS THINKING

Since the tune is in the key of Bb, the soloist uses Bb major or sliding scales through most of the chord changes. Scales that relate directly to each chord change are often played. (For example, an Ebm scale with an Ebm6 chord) Following the solo are notes explaining each substitute scale that is used.

SIMPLIFIED PROGRESSION

Key of Bb ‖: Bb | BbM7 | Bb7 |·/·| EbM7 |·/·| Ebm6 |·/·| BbM7 |·/·| C7 |·/·| Cm |G7 |Cm |F7 :‖ F7 | Bb |·/·‖

[1. Cm | G7] [2. F7 | Bb |·/·]

Bridge: ‖C#m |F#7 |BM7 |·/·| Bm | E7 |AM7 |·/·| Am |D7 |GM7 |·/·| Gm | C7 | F7 |·/·‖ (Repeat verse with 2nd ending)

CHEROKEE

Written and Composed by
RAY NOBLE

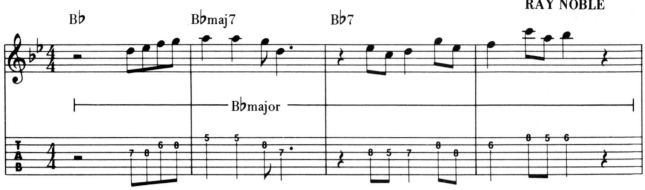

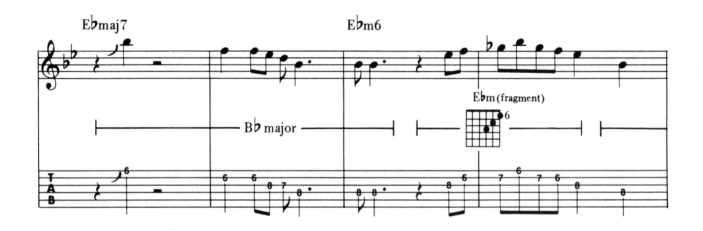

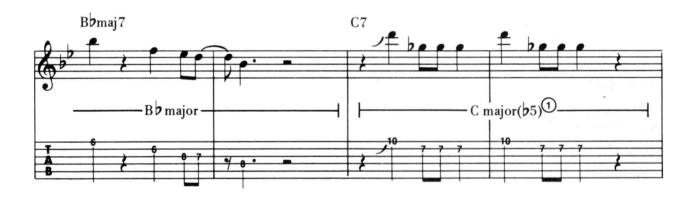

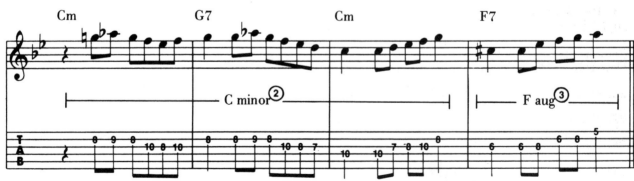

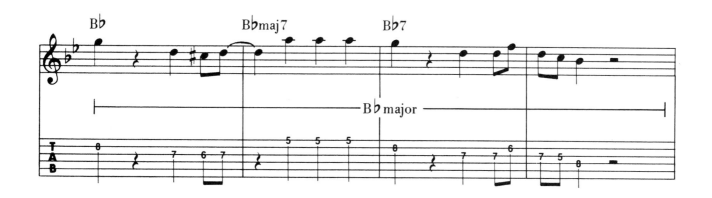

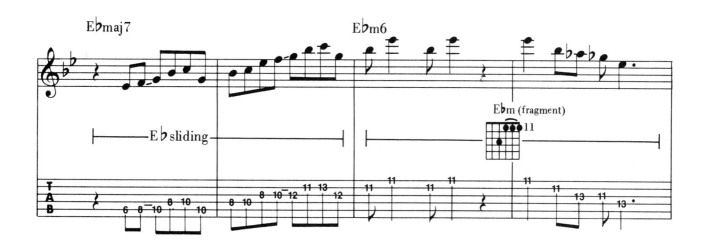

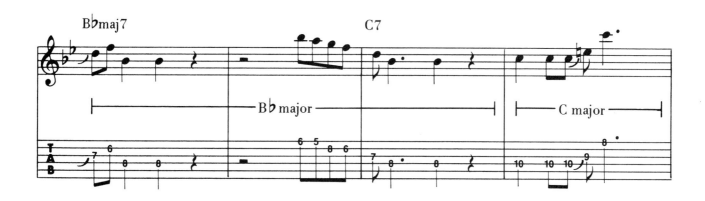

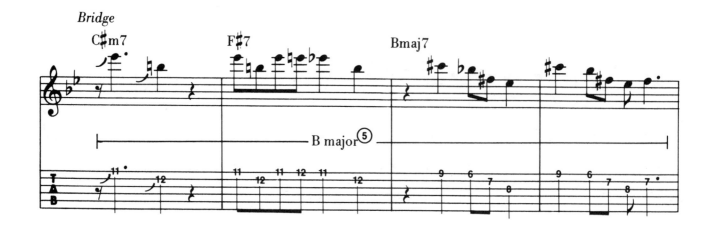

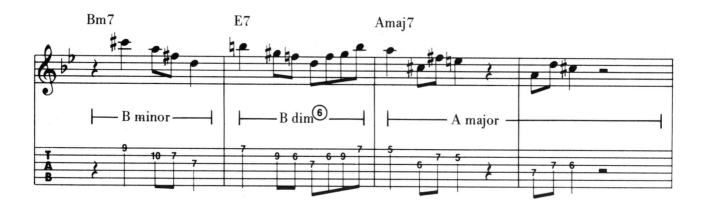

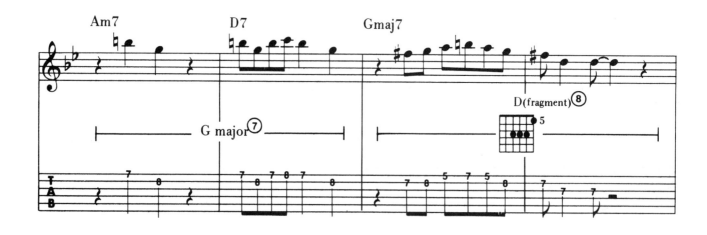

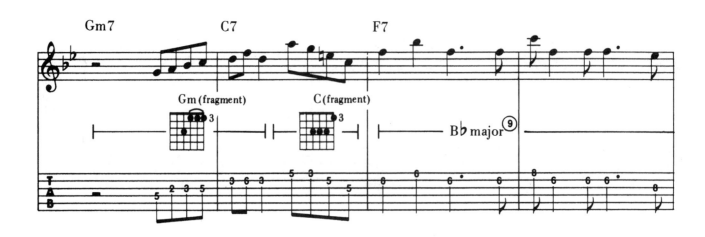

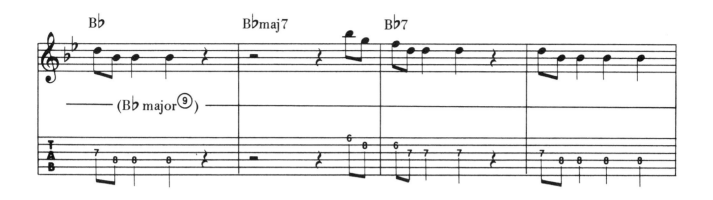

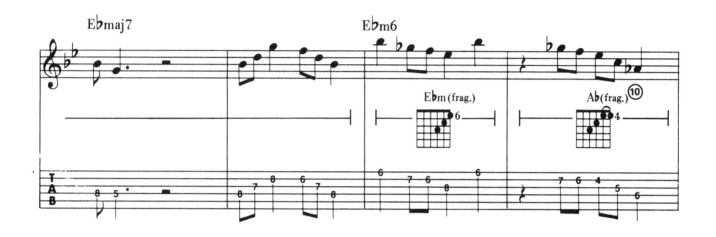

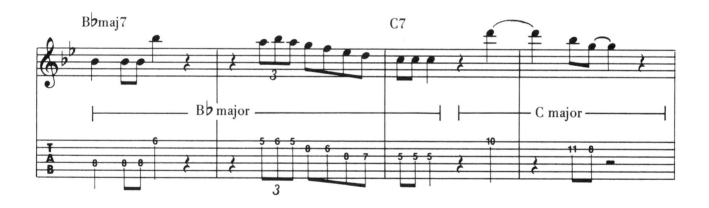

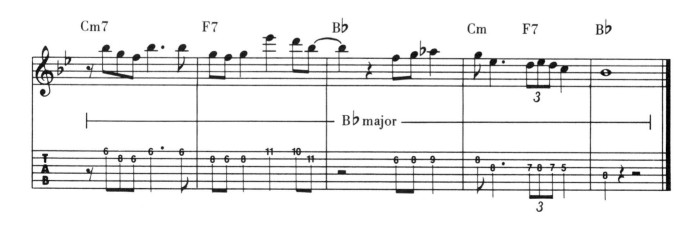

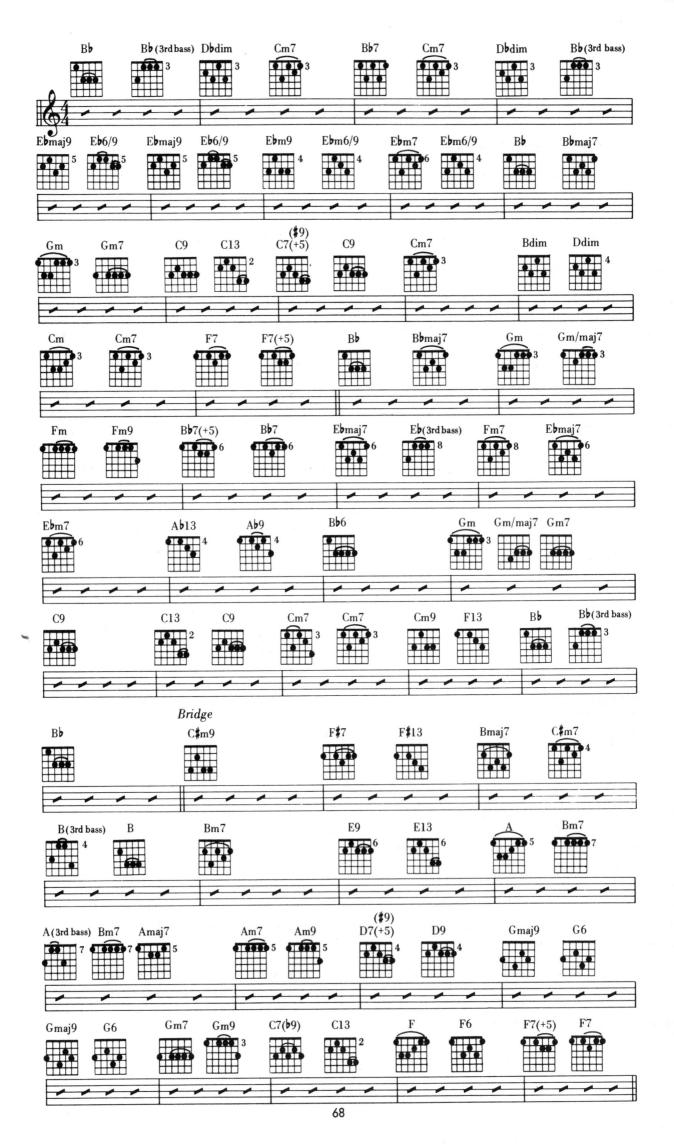

NOTES ON SCALE SUBSTITUTIONS

1) For variety, a ♭5 is added to the C scale.

2) The Cm scale works with the G7 chord because of the reverse dominant minor substitution rule.

3) The F+ scale resolves a 4th higher, to the B♭.

4) The B♭ sliding scale works well with this 2-5-1 progression (Cm, F7, B♭).

5) Using B as the key center, the soloist plays B major scales with the 2-5-1 changes.

6) B♭° scales work with an E7 chord by the diminished substitution rules (see p. 66, first par.)

7) As in note 5), the soloist regards Am7-D7-GM7 as a 2-5-1 progression in the key of G, and plays G major scales.

8) At the G (tonic) a D scale (a 5th above G) is played. See the Major 9 Scale Substitution rule on p. 67.

9) The soloist anticipates the B♭ chord and plays B♭ scales with the F7.

10) The A♭ scale is a reverse dominant minor substitution for E♭m6.

BACK-UP GUITAR: COMMENTARY AND NOTES

The swing guitarists in the big bands of the '20's and '30's "comped" in a very regular, one-chord-for-every-beat fashion. Though the rhythm seldom varied, they constantly improvised with chords, often playing a different chord on each beat. A typical "comping" rhythm is written out below, and is played on the recording as the "CHEROKEE" accompaniment. Note the extensive use of scalewise (and other) substitutes.

CHARLIE'S BLUES

Music by FRED SOKOLOW

SIMPLIFIED PROGRESSION

Key of G ‖ G7 | C9 | G | G9 | CM7 | C#° | G C | Bm7 E7 | A7 | D9 | G E7 | A7 D7 ‖

HIGHLIGHTS OF THE PROGRESSION

This is typical of the 12-bar blues progression played by a swing band of the '30's or early '40's. Compare these changes to the basic 12-bar blues in G:

‖ G | C7 | G7 | ·/· | C7 | ·/· | G7 | ·/· | D7 | ·/· | G7 | D7 ‖

A circle of 5ths begins in the 8th measure. (The C in the 7th measure leads to the Bm7, which begins the circle.) Once the cycle resolves to G, a quick turnaround follows (E7, A7, D7) to end the progression.

There are infinite ways to vary the 12-bar blues by adding diminished chords or dominant minor substitutions, and "cycling back" in the circle of 5ths. "CHARLIE'S BLUES" is one of these variations.

HOW THE SOLOIST IS THINKING

G blues scales and G and C major scales comprise most of the solo. In the Charlie Christian style, many diminished scales are added for variety. In a blues, of course, G blues scales can be used with all the changes.

CHARLIE'S BLUES

Music by
FRED SOKOLOW

Moderate Swing

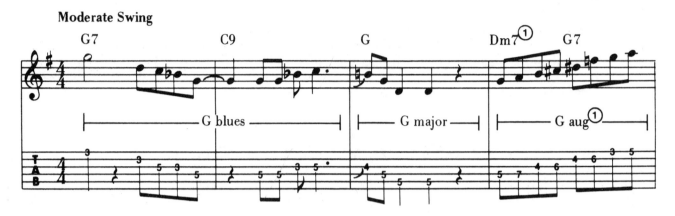

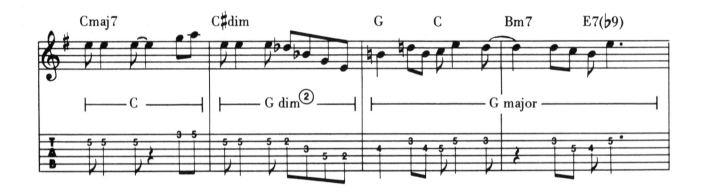

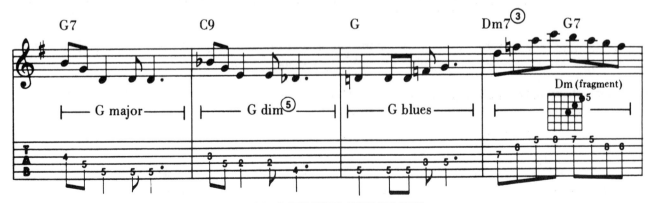

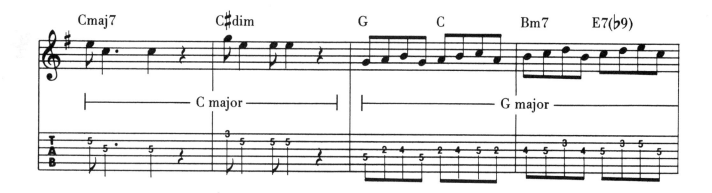

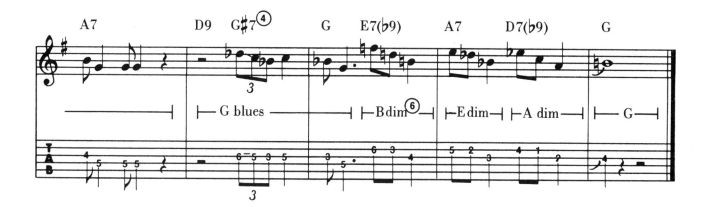

NOTES ON SCALE SUBSTITUTIONS

1) The G+ scale resolves to the CM7 chord, a typical use of the augmented scale.

2) The G° scale duplicates the C#° scale (see p. 63, diminished scales).

3) E° is a substitute for A7, according to the diminished substitution rules (see p. 23, on ♭9 chord substitution).

4) The same as 3), A° scales work with a D9 chord.

5) The same as 3), G° scales work with a C9 chord.

6) The B°, E° and A° scales all follow the same rule as 3). Each scale starts a fret below the previous one. This series of descending scales adds interest to the common 6-2-5-1 turnaround.

BACK-UP GUITAR: COMMENTARY AND NOTES

This back-up is slightly looser, rhythmically, than "CHEROKEE'S" accompaniment, but the same basic chord-on-every-beat feeling is achieved. All substitute chords are noted:

1) Dm7 is a dominant minor substitution for G7.

2) G#7 is a ♭5 substitution for D9, as well as a passing chord that leads to G.

3) The same as 1).

4) The same as 2).

WILLOW WEEP FOR ME

Composed by ANN RONELL

SIMPLIFIED PROGRESSION

Key of C ‖: C9 F9 |·/·|·/·| C9 | F9 | Dm11 G7 | C9 F9 |⌐1.⌐ C9 G9 :‖ ⌐2.⌐ C7 ‖

Bridge: ‖: Fm | Cm C7 | Fm Eb7 |⌐1.⌐ Db7 C7 :‖ ⌐2.⌐ Db7 G9 :‖ (repeat verse with 1st ending)

HIGHLIGHTS OF THE PROGRESSION

1-4 movement (C-F) encompasses most of the verse.

2-5-1 movement also occurs in the verse. (Dm11-G7-C9).

The bridge (in the key of Fm) contains a Spanish-sounding minor-key progression: Fm-Eb7-Db7-C7. This is a scalewise (downward) progression.

A b5 jump (Db-G) in the 2nd ending of the bridge, brings the tune back to the key of C.

HOW THE SOLOIST IS THINKING

The soloist treats the verse like a blues, using mainly C blues scales, C sliding and C major scales over all the changes. During the rapid chord changes of the bridge, "fragment" scales are employed. Since a medium-tempo swing or shuffle-beat, such as this, is the same as a sped-up 12/8 beat, the soloist uses triplets to create 12-beat measures. (1-2-3-4, in 4/4 time, is similar to 1-2-3 2-2-3 3-2-3 4-2-3, 12/8 time.)

WILLOW WEEP FOR ME

Composed by
ANN RONELL

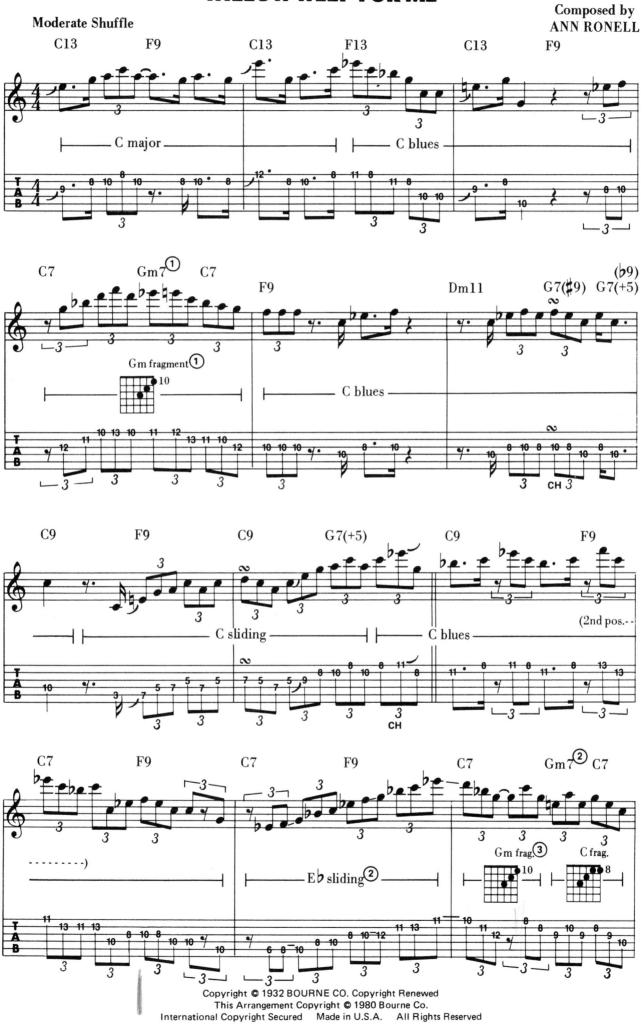

74

OTES ON SCALE SUBSTITUTIONS

1) The Gm scale works with the C7 chords because of the dominant minor substitution rule.

2) The E♭ sliding scale works because of the "relative major sliding scale" substitution rule. (See p. 66.)

3) The same as 1).

4) G♯ is a ♭5 substitution for Dm7♭5. (See p. 67 on m7♭5 substitutions.)

5) The D sliding scale works with a C+11 chord. (See p. 67 on +11 substitutions.)

BACK-UP GUITAR: COMMENTARY AND NOTES

This accompaniment is more contemporary than those of the first two tunes. In this typical shuffle beat, the guitarist does not chop out one chord per beat, nor does he or she repeat a rhythm pattern. Instead, he or she adds chords in an unpredictable, sparse, improvisational way that punctuates the beat. He or she listens to, and complements the bass and drums. Also, a more modern sound is achieved by extending the given chords, that is, by adding 9ths, 13ths, etc.

1) Cm7 is a dominant minor substitution for C7.

2) The same as 1).

3) The same as 1).

4) The B♭7 and A♭13 are added to make the bridge more interesting. B♭7 is a reverse dominant minor substitution for Fm7. A♭13 bears the same relation to E♭m9.

5) The same as 1).

YOU ARE SO BEAUTIFUL

Lyric and Music by BILLY PRESTON & BRUCE FISHER

SIMPLIFIED PROGRESSION

Key of F ‖ F FM7 F7 | B♭M7 B♭m6 | F B♭ | F C7sus | F FM7 F7 | B♭M7 B♭m6 | F | Cm F7 | B♭ | A7 | Dm ¦ G9 B♭m6 |

F FM7 F7 | B♭M7 B♭m6 | F B♭ | F C7sus ‖

HIGHLIGHTS OF THE PROGRESSION

The tune is basically a 1-4-4m-1 turnaround (F, B♭, B♭m, F) repeated several times.

A 3-6-2-5-1 cycle occurs in the middle of the tune (starting with the A7), with B♭m6 substituted for the 5 chord (C).

A typical false cadence ending has been added.

On the recording, the first 8 measures are played in "double-time", so that they become 16 measures.

HOW THE SOLOIST IS THINKING

These blues changes, with a circle of 5ths added, are often called "gospel changes" since they never stray far from the tonic; the soloist plays mostly in F. (F blues, F major and F sliding scales are used.)

YOU ARE SO BEAUTIFUL

Lyric and Music by
BILLY PRESTON
and BRUCE FISHER

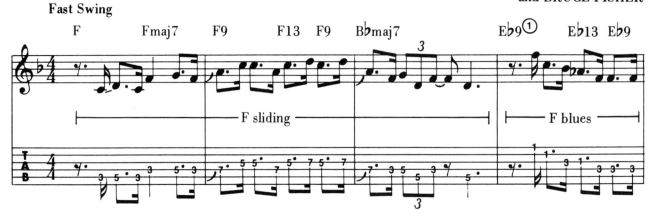

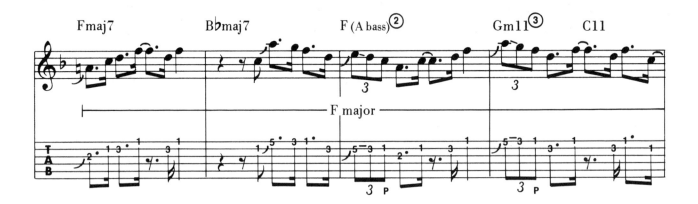

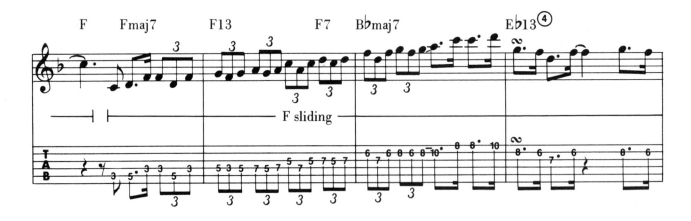

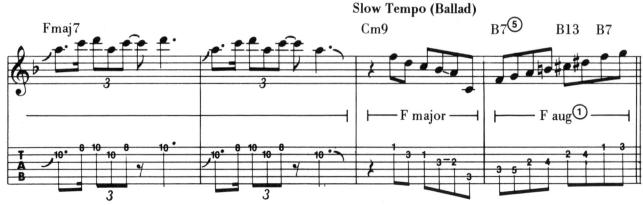

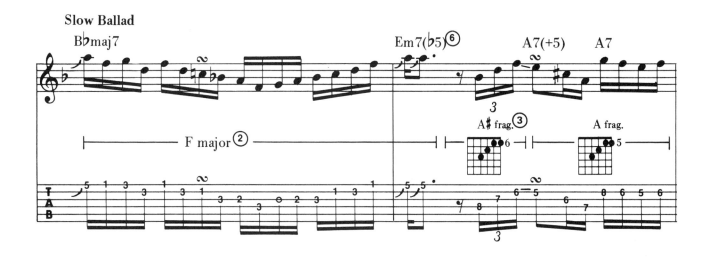

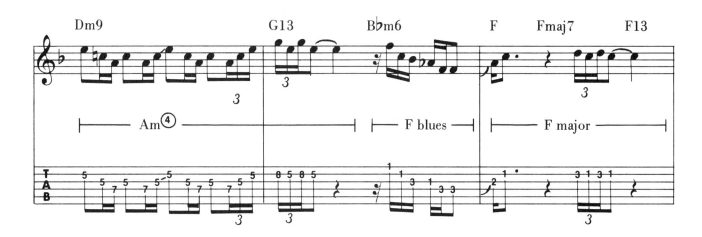

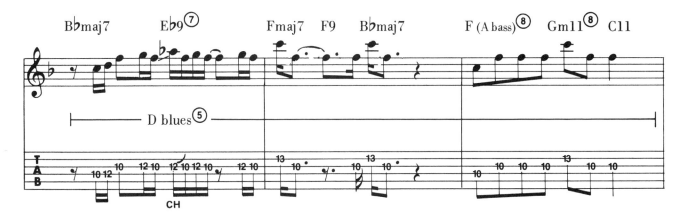

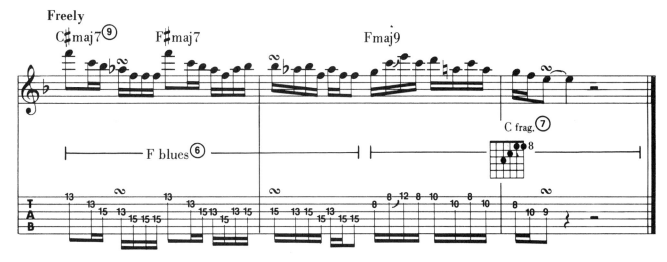

OTES ON SCALE SUBSTITUTIONS

1) The F+ scale resolves a 4th higher, to B♭. It works with the substituted B7 chord as well, since B+ and F+ scales contain the same notes.

2) The F major scale works well with the B♭M7 chord. (See p. 67 on "Major 9th Chord Substitution.")

3) The A♯ scale is a ♭5 substitution for Em7♭5. (See p. 67 on "Half-Diminished Chord Scale Substitution.")

4) The Am scale is a dominant minor substitution for Dm9. (See p. 67).

5) The D blues scale works in the key of F because of the relative minor blues scale substitution rule (p. 67).

6) The tonic (F) blues scale works well with false cadence chords.

7) Here is another example of M9 scale substitution.

ACK-UP GUITAR: COMMENTARY AND NOTES

As in "WILLOW WEEP FOR ME", guitar comping is sketchy and irregular. Chords are often extended to achieve a more modern sound.

1) E♭7 substitutes for B♭m6 by the reverse dominant minor substitution rule.

2) The F is played with an A in the bass to create a descending bass line in the B♭-F/A-Gm11 sequence.

3) Gm11 is a dominant minor substitution for C11.

4) The same as 1).

5) B7, a ♭5 substitution for F7, resolves to B♭.

6) Em7♭5 is a dominant minor substitution for A7.

7) The same as 1).

8) The same as 2) and 3).

9) This chord begins the false cadence ending.

EVERYTHING MUST CHANGE

Lyric and Music by BENARD IGHNER

SIMPLIFIED PROGRESSION

Key of Gm ‖: Gm │ D+ (F♯ bass) │ B♭ (F bass) │ Em7♭5 │ E♭M7 Dm7 │ Cm7 Cm7 (B♭ bass) │ Am7♭5 │ D7 :‖ ⌐1.┐ A♭M7 │ F7sus ‖ ⌐2.┐

Bridge: ‖ B♭M7 │ Am7♭5 D7 │ Gm7 │ C9 │ E♭M7 │ B♭ (D bass) │ Cm7 │ D7♯9 │·/· ‖ Start Over

HIGHLIGHTS OF THE PROGRESSION

The descending minor progression (Gm, Gm/M7, Gm7, etc.) appears here in chordal form. (See p. 20).

Scalewise movement: The descending notes of the minor progression continue down the scale for another bar to the Am7♭5 chord. Another descending progression occurs in the bridge (Measures 5, 6 & 7).

2-5-1 movement, in the 1st ending of the verse, resolves to Gm. Circle of 5ths movement also appears in the bridge (Am7♭5-D7-Gm7-C9).

The tune is in Gm, but it occasionally shifts, momentarily, to the relative major key (B♭), for example, the bridge starts in B♭.

HOW THE SOLOIST IS THINKING

Since the key is Gm, the Gm, G blues and B♭ scales (major and sliding) work throughout all the changes. Instead of varying the solo with substitution scales, the soloist plays rhythmic, bluesy clichés, common to the jazz-rock genré. The R&B rhythm section naturally lends itself to a funky, R&B-oriented soloing style.

EVERYTHING MUST CHANGE

Lyric and Music by
BENARD IGHNER

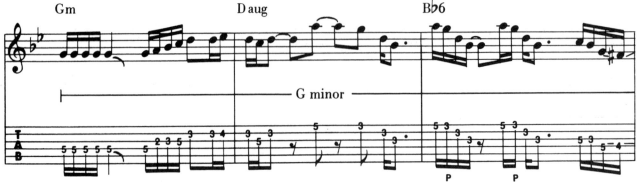

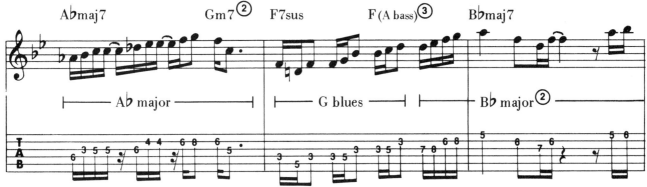

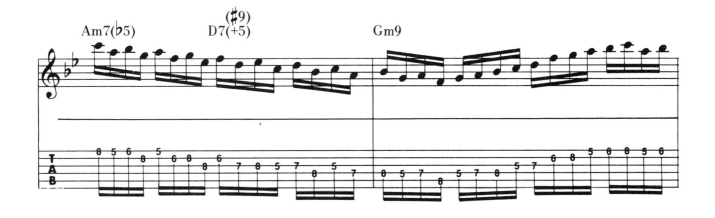

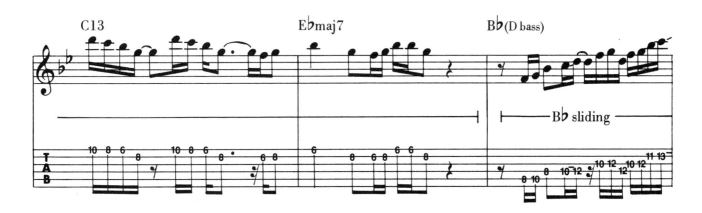

NOTES ON SCALE SUBSTITUTIONS

1) The E+ scale works with an Eb5 chord (see p. 66 augmented scale substitution).

2) The Bb major "practice scale" (G major scale Ex. A on p. 55 is used here.) A Bb major scale contains the same notes as its relative minor (Gm), and Am-D7 is 2-5 (-1) to the key of Gm.

BACK-UP GUITAR: COMMENTARY AND NOTES

To achieve an R&B "groove," a back-up guitarist plays funky rhythmic *patterns* that fit the bass and drum rhythm scheme. He or she maintains one repetitious pattern throughout a whole section of a tune, or even throughout the whole tune. Here are some rhythm patterns that fit this particular "groove". The 1st one is heard during the verse and first part of the bridge, the 2nd is played starting from the 5th measure of the bridge.

Arrows indicate right-hand pick movement.

1) E9b5 substitutes for the Em7b5 more commonly heard in this minor progression.

2) Gm7 is a passing chord between AbM7 and F7sus. It creates a downward scalewise progression.

3) The F(A bass) is a scalewise bridge from F7sus to BbM7.

 # OCTAVE SOLOING

Octave soloing was most recently popularized by Wes Montgomery. But long before Wes, Django Reinhardt and other jazz guitarists used octaves to emphasize a melody line, to effect a fuller sound or to create punctuated rhythmic patterns.

In the following octave positions the player must mute the "in-between" string with the index finger of his left hand.

     or

"Double-Octaves"

I= index
L= little finger
M= middle
R= ring

These single note scales have been adapted for octave playing. Play them ascending and descending:

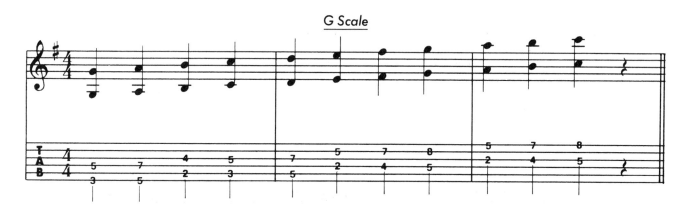

G Scale

Any single-note scale can be adapted for octave use. Go back to the single-note scale exercises and solos and play them all in the octave style.

George Benson has developed an octave technique that includes a harmony note. His finger positions differ from those above.

Starting with this octave... add one of these notes.   Starting with this octave... add one of these notes.

Pick the bass string with a flatpick (or the thumb) and use one or two fingers to pluck the treble strings. This will be easier than muting the extra string.

Notice the use of these harmony notes in the bridge to "WE'VE ONLY JUST BEGUN."

WE'VE ONLY JUST BEGUN

Lyric by PAUL WILLIAMS
Music by ROGER NICHOLS

SIMPLIFIED PROGRESSION

Key of Eb ‖: EbM7 | AbM7 | Gm7 | Cm7 | Fm7 | Cm7 | Fm7 | Bb7 :‖ [1.] Bb7 | EbM7 AbM7 | [2.] EbM7 AbM7 G7 ‖

Bridge: ‖ CM7 FM7 | ·/· | ·/· | ·/· | EM7 AM7 | ·/· | ·/· | Bb7 | ·/· ‖

HIGHLIGHTS OF THE PROGRESSION

Relative minor key changes occur in the verse—back and forth from Eb to its relative minor, Cm.

6-2-5-1 movement occurs in the verse (Cm7-Fm7-Bb7-EbM7).

1-4 movement makes up the bridge (C-F and E-A).

This version of the tune is played double-time. Each measure is stretched to two measures.

HOW THE SOLOIST IS THINKING

Notice the rhythmic quality of the solo. Since the octave style lends itself to a simpler melodic line than single-note soloing, a heavier rhythmic line is played. The interesting rhythmic device in Measures 13—16 was often used by Wes Montgomery. During the bridge, the soloist plays the octaves with an extra note added, as explained on p. 91.

WE'VE ONLY JUST BEGUN

Lyric by
PAUL WILLIAMS

Music by
ROGER NICHOLS

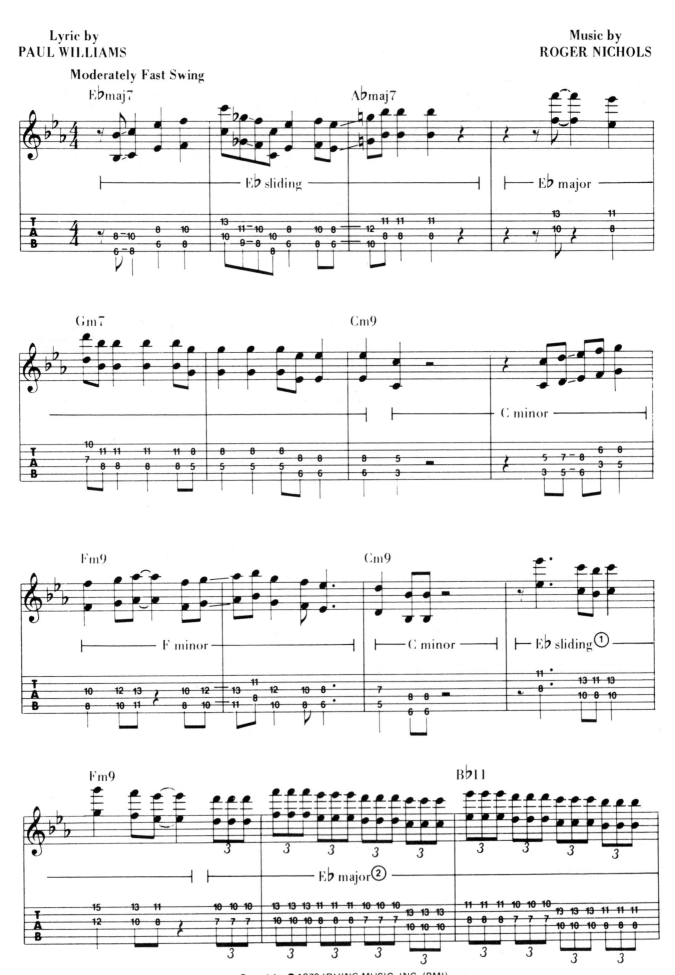

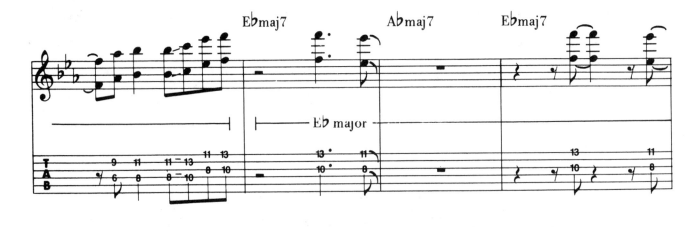

Bridge

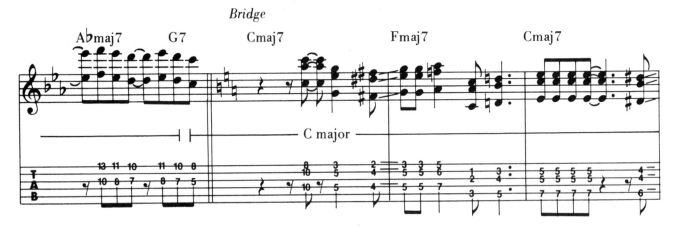

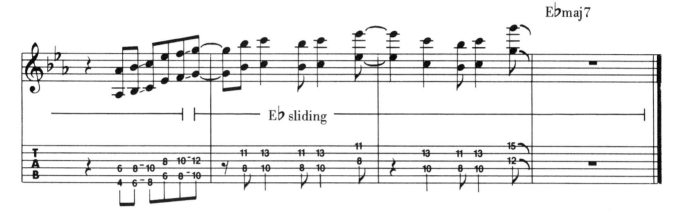

NOTES ON SCALE SUBSTITUTIONS

1) The Eb sliding scale works with a Cm9 chord since Eb is the relative major to Cm. It works with the Fm9 chord because of the dominant minor substitution principle (p. 67).

2) Fm9-Bb11 is 2-5 to the key of Eb, so an Eb major scale works with these chords. The solo line here imitates one of the major scale exercises (p. 55, G major scale Ex. B).

3) The Gm scale works with the Cm9, as well as the Gm7, because of the dominant minor rule mentioned in 1).

4) The next several measures quote the old tune, "I'M GONNA SIT RIGHT DOWN AND WRITE MYSELF A LETTER."

5) The Ab sliding scale works with the Bb11 because of the 11th chord substitution rule (p. 67).

6) The same as 5).

BACK-UP GUITAR: COMMENTARY

This is the same style back up as in "WILLOW WEEP FOR ME" and "YOU ARE SO BEAUTIFUL". Rhythm chops are sparse, follow no particular repeated pattern, and serve mainly to enhance the rhythm.

GLOSSARY OF CHORD SYMBOLS

There is no absolute standard notation for chord symbols. Here are some variations in common use:

G minor 7= Gm7, G-7, Gmi7

G7 augmented 5= G7+ , G7+5, G7♯5, G7aug

G7 flat 5= G7−5, G7♭5

G major 7= GMAJ7, Gmaj7, GM7, G△ , G△7, Gma7

G diminished= G°, G− , G7− , Gdim

G minor 7♭5= G⌀ , G half-diminished, Gm7♭5

G six, add 9= G6,9, G6/9, G6add9, G$_9^6$

G augmented 11= G+11, G11+ , Gaug11

G (F bass)= G/F

HORD DICTIONARY

This dictionary divides chord formations into four basic types: major, dominant 7th, minor and diminished. Variations of these basic types are arranged numerically; for example, minor 7th precedes minor 9th.

Every chord pictured is a moveable formation. The root note of each chord is circled. To play any chord, fret the formation with the root on the desired note.

Several voicings can be found for every chord. Using Bbm7b5 as an example, follow these steps:

1. Locate minor chords.
2. Find m7b5 (between m6/9 and m/M7).
3. Play the circled note as Bb.

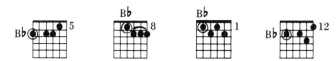

Context determines the correct voicing. In a chord solo, choose the voicing that contains, or is nearest to, the melody note. For comping (playing back-up chords) choose the voicing nearest on the fingerboard to the last chord played. When playing a scalewise progression, that progression will determine the appropriate voicing. To create a feeling of dynamic change, or to make a chord stand out, select a voicing with a noticeably higher pitch than the preceding chords.

Some chords in the dictionary are played with the thumb on the 6th string. Guitarists who find this kind of fingering awkward, may play an alternative form. For example:

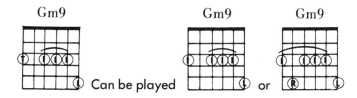

CHORD DICTIONARY

MAJOR CHORD GROUP

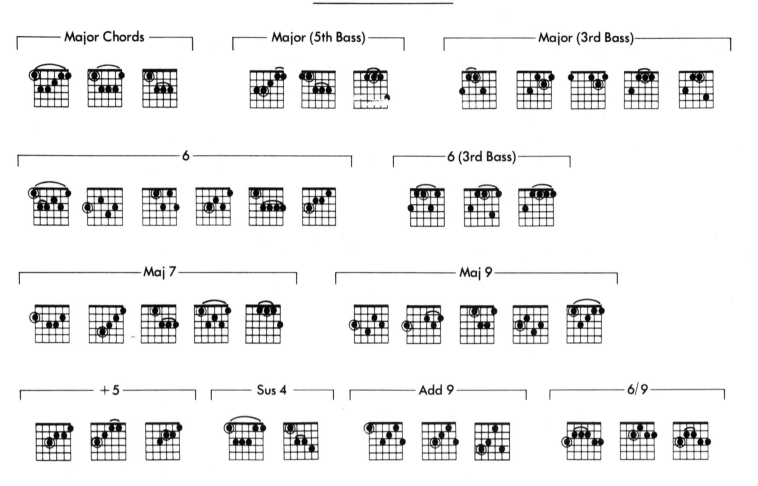

Major Chords — Major (5th Bass) — Major (3rd Bass)

6 — 6 (3rd Bass)

Maj 7 — Maj 9

+5 — Sus 4 — Add 9 — 6/9

DOMINANT 7th CHORD GROUP

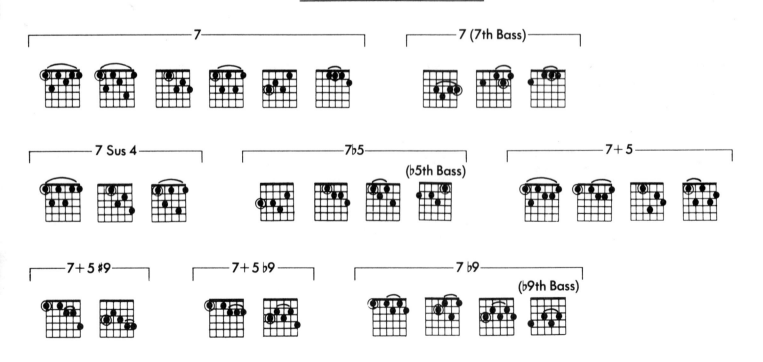

7 — 7 (7th Bass)

7 Sus 4 — 7b5 (b5th Bass) — 7+5

7+5 #9 — 7+5 b9 — 7 b9 (b9th Bass)

DOMINANT 7th CHORD GROUP CONTINUED

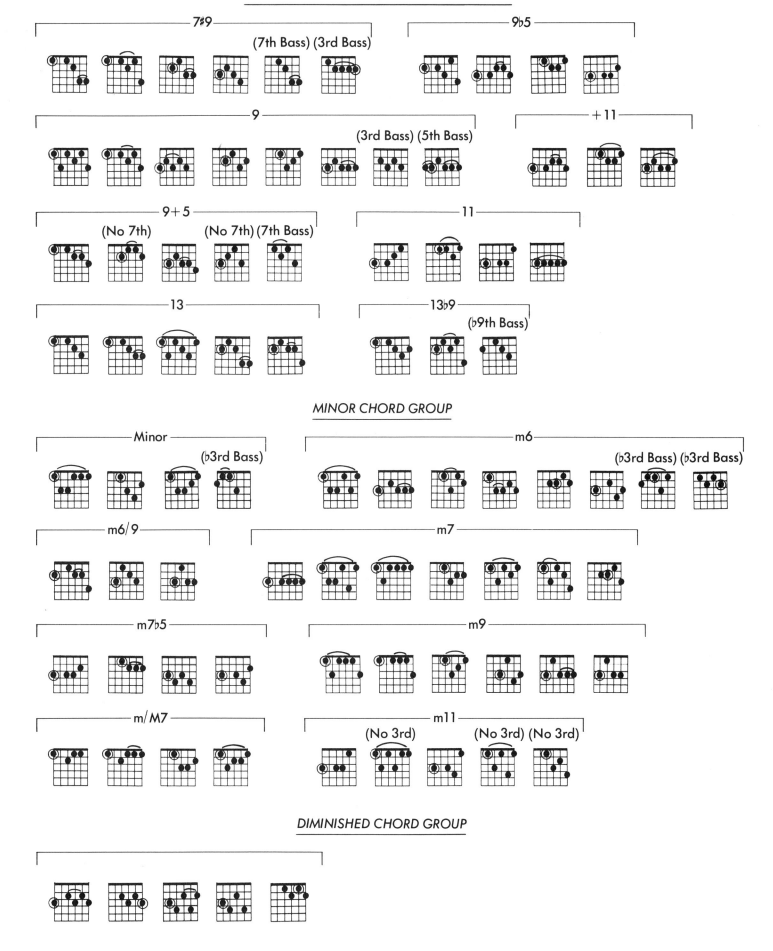

DISCOGRAPHY: WHO TO LISTEN TO

Most jazz guitarists and critics will agree that three names stand out in jazz guitar history: Django Reinhardt, Charlie Christian and Wes Montgomery. They are the most innovative and the most imitated stylists.

Django Reinhardt was a Belgian gypsy who rose to fame playing swing music in France in the '30's. His improvisation, mostly single-note and octave solos, is brilliant, unique and fresh sounding, even though his recordings are 50 years old!

Charlie Christian was the first definitive electric jazz guitarist. He played with Benny Goodman at the end of the '30's and in the early '40's. His amplified single-note solos used new-sounding scales and leading tones which were indicative of the bop movement that was just beginning.

Wes Montgomery popularized a warm, full, octave-soloing style in the '60's. He also played brilliant chord solos and single-note solos using a horn player's improvisational approach.

Rhythm and Blues roots are evident in Charlie's and Wes' playing. Kenny Burrell, George Benson and Grant Green are three other excellent jazz guitarists with an R&B feel. Other contemporary guitarists noted for excellent chord and single-note soloing are Barney Kessel, Tal Farlow, Johnny Smith, Howard Roberts and Joe Pass. These players are all in the mainstream of jazz music and have played with some of the best bands of the last few decades.

To hear swing-style guitar back-up (as in the "CHEROKEE" example) listen to the "guitar giant" records that pair up Herb Ellis, Joe Pass, Barney Kessel and Charlie Byrd in various combinations. This back-up style was best exemplified by Freddie Green (of Count Basie's band) and other big-band guitarists, the back-up guitar is easier to pick out in these duet or trio records.

For beautiful acoustic guitar chord solos, listen to Laurindo Almeida, Charlie Byrd, Bola Sete.

In the more modern vein (jazz guitarists experimenting with new scale-ideas, polytonal jazz, and rock sounds) listen to Pat Martino, George Benson, Larry Coryell, Lee Ritenour, John McLaughlin and Al Dimeola.